WORLD WAR II FROM ORIGINAL SOURCES

ARNHEM 1944
A BRIDGE TOO FAR?

EDITED AND INTRODUCED
BY BOB CARRUTHERS

Pen & Sword

This edition published in 2013 by
Pen & Sword Military
An imprint of
Pen & Sword Books Ltd
47 Church Street
Barnsley
South Yorkshire
S70 2AS

First published in Great Britain in 2011 in digital format by
Coda Books Ltd.

ISBN 978 1 78159 237 3

A CIP catalogue record for this book is
available from the British Library

Printed and bound by CPI group (UK) Ltd, Croydon, CR0 4YY

Pen & Sword Books Ltd incorporates the Imprints of Pen & Sword Aviation, Pen &
Sword Family History, Pen & Sword Maritime, Pen & Sword Military, Pen &
Sword Discovery, Pen & Sword Politics, Pen & Sword Atlas, Pen & Sword
Archaeology, Wharncliffe Local History, Wharncliffe True Crime, Wharncliffe
Transport, Pen & Sword Select, Pen & Sword Military Classics, Leo Cooper, The
Praetorian Press, Claymore Press, Remember When, Seaforth Publishing and
Frontline Publishing

For a complete list of Pen & Sword titles please contact
PEN & SWORD BOOKS LIMITED
47 Church Street, Barnsley, South Yorkshire, S70 2AS, England
E-mail: enquiries@pen-and-sword.co.uk
Website: www.pen-and-sword.co.uk

CONTENTS

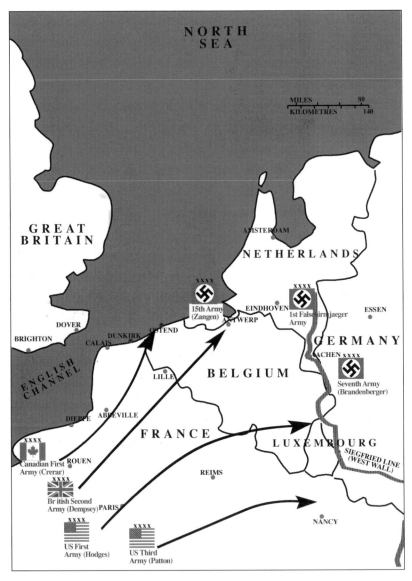

THE STRATEGIC SITUATION SEPTEMBER 15TH 1944.
In September 1944 the German forces in the west were spread very thinly indeed, and it was the tantalising gap which appeared between 15th Army and 7th Army which led Montgomery to the conclusion that a single narrow thrust towards Berlin could be mounted through the low countries.

INTRODUCTION
OPERATION MARKET-GARDEN

The complex set of operations played out in the Netherlands during September 1944 involved the forces of Britain, Canada, Poland, the USA and Germany. As far as space permits we have attempted to provide a wide selection of sources covering each of the belligerents.

We are also proud to present the previously unpublished war diary of Captain Graham Davies which brings a new perspective on the often overlooked contribution made by the artillerymen in support of both Operation Market and Operation Garden.

The German perspective is covered by the contemporary newspaper account filed by Erwin Kirchhof, which provides a powerful insight into the events of the battle as filtered through the prism of Goebel's propaganda machine.

We also include two extracts from the official accounts of the 101st Airborne and 82nd Airborne which give an indication of the strong conviction held in the US camp that the operation had been a complete success.

Finally, we present an extract from the official account of the British First and Sixth Airborne Divisions, showing the British point of view of the battle of Arnhem.

CHAPTER ONE

OPERATION MARKET-GARDEN

The Strategic Situation

Following the crushing defeat in Normandy in July to August 1944, the shattered remnants of German forces withdrew across the Low Countries and eastern France towards the German border. By the end of August the Germans had been cleared from almost all of Northern France. In the north during the first week of September, the British 21st Army Group under Field Marshal Bernard Montgomery was advancing on a line running from Antwerp to the northern border of Belgium. The advance was led by the British Second Army under Lieutenant-General Sir Miles Dempsey while its First Canadian Army under Lieutenant-General Harry Crerar had commenced its task of recapturing the ports of Dieppe, Le Havre and Boulogne-sur-Mer.

To the south, the U.S. 12th Army Group under Lieutenant General Omar Bradley was nearing the German border and had been ordered to focus on the Aachen gap with Lieutenant General Courtney Hodges' U.S. First Army in support of Montgomery's advance on the Ruhr, the U.S. Third Army under Lieutenant General George S. Patton was moving eastward towards the Saar. Finally the U.S. 6th Army Group under General Jacob L. Devers was advancing north east towards Germany after their landings in southern France.

In the north Allied supply sources were still limited to the original invasion beaches, the nearby deep water port of Cherbourg at the tip of the Cotentin peninsula and some minor ports in Normandy. These sources had been adequate for the campaign in Normandy however as the Allied pursuit across France and Belgium continued the lines soon became over extended, a situation which was compounded by soaring fuel consumption as the armies moved further north and eastwards. By 28th August the situation was becoming critical and Communications Zone reported it could no longer guarantee fuel deliveries. Both the US First and Third Armies reported less than a day's supply on hand.

There was some prospect of salvation when the massive port of Antwerp was captured by Montgomery's troops on September 4, but frustratingly much of the Scheldt estuary leading to the port still remained under German control. Other important ports on the English Channel coast such as Dunkirk were never captured during the war and in fact remained in German hands until the surrender in May 1945. Although over-the-beach supply operations in Normandy outperformed all expectations, September 1944 brought deteriorating weather conditions and rising seas. The effectiveness of expedient measures such as the Mulberry Harbour was clearly in sight. Deep-water ports were therefore required. The Overlord plan had foreseen this, calling for the exploitation of ports in Brittany and Eisenhower sticking slavishly to the plan persisted with his efforts to capture the Brittany ports despite the fact that the shift in focus of the campaign made the capture of strong points such as Le Havre even more unnecessary.

Although in terms of volume there were enough supplies being landed to support Allied operations, it was the desperate shortage of transport to move these supplies forward which was creating a bottleneck. In an effort to ease the transport situation the advancing divisions of the US 12th Army Group were forced to leave all their heavy artillery and half their medium artillery west of the Seine in order to free their trucks to move supplies for infantry units. Four British truck companies were also loaned to the Americans. The creation of the famous Red Ball Express supply route did much to lessen the impact of the transport shortage but this ad hoc operation could not solve the overall strategic problem.

Railway transport was the obvious solution and represented by far the most economical form of transport but the allies own efforts had contributed to their own downfall in this respect. The pre-invasion air strikes had badly damaged the rail lines and destroyed huge numbers of locomotives. The frantic reconstruction effort could simply not keep pace. By the end of August, 18,000 men, including 5,000 prisoners of war, were engaged on railway construction projects. Fortunately, the system had not been nearly so badly damaged east of the Seine and after many delays, the first trainload of supplies reached the US Third Army depot at Le Mans on 17 August.

The British 21st Army Group were equally hard pressed and resorted to the expedient of stripping two of it's divisions of their transport. With supplies continuing to pile up at the ports they simply could not be moved fast enough, the result was chaos in the docks and on 30th August the decision was taken to suspend imports entirely. In the meantime it was ordered that 21st Army Group would draw on its reserve supplies in Normandy until the more northerly ports of Dieppe and Boulogne-sur-Mer could be opened. This difficult situation was exacerbated by the fact that 1,400 British three-ton trucks were found to be useless because of faulty pistons in their engines — these vehicles could otherwise have moved 800 tons per day, enough for two entire divisions.

The Allied Strategy

Following the British and Canadian breakout from Caen and the closure of the Falaise pocket, General Dwight D. Eisenhower, Supreme Commander of the Allied Expeditionary Force, favoured pursuit of the battered German armies eastwards to the Rhine on the broadest possible front. He agreed however that Montgomery's drive towards the Ruhr should have priority. Eisenhower also maintained that it was important to get Patton and his stalled forces moving again as soon as possible. In the first week of September 1944, Eisenhower therefore authorised the First Army to cross the Rhine near Cologne, Bonn and Koblenz while the Third Army crossed near Mannheim, Mainz and Karlsruhe. Eisenhower was relying upon on a speedy advance but this placed even more strain on the hard pushed logistics services which even Eisenhower now conceded were stretched to the limit.

The expansive front strategy made life even more difficult for the formations fighting the north and was fiercely contested by Montgomery, who argued that with the supply situation deteriorating, he would not be able to reach the Ruhr on a broad front. Instead he argued for a narrow thrust up the road corridor through Holland and stated that "a relocation of our present resources of every description would be adequate to get one thrust to Berlin".

Operation Comet

Following their successful deployment in Normandy the allied airborne forces had been withdrawn to rest and refit in England and in the process had been formed into the First Allied Airborne Army which comprised two British, three U.S. airborne divisions and a Polish brigade. The First Allied Airborne Army had been created on 16th August as the result of repeated British requests for a coordinated headquarters for airborne operations. The concept was approved by General Eisenhower on 20th June. British hopes that Browning, the most obvious British candidate for commander, would be appointed its first commander were soon dashed. Eisenhower took the reasonable view that as the bulk of both troops and aircraft were American, then an American should be in overall command. Brereton, a U.S. Army Air Force officer, was formally named acting commander by Eisenhower on 16th July and was duly appointed by SHAEF on 2nd August. As the British pointed out a great length, Brereton had no experience in airborne operations, Eisenhower countered that he did have extensive command experience at the air force level which had been gained in several theatres, above all he had most recently been commander of Ninth Air Force, which gave him a working knowledge of the operations of IX Troop Carrier Command.

Despite the squabbling over command, the fact remained that this highly trained and effective force was completely underutilized. In deference to SHAEF this unhappy situation was clearly not for the want of trying. Following the battle for Normandy, plans for eighteen airborne operations had been drafted and approved only to be cancelled at short notice, usually as a result of Allied ground forces overrunning the intended objectives.

Montgomery was all too aware of this large and highly trained paratroop force which was available to him. He therefore proposed Operation Comet, a limited airborne operation that was to be launched on 2nd September 1944. Comet envisioned using the British 1st Airborne Division, along with the Polish 1st Independent Parachute Brigade. The plan was to secure several bridges over the River Rhine to aid the Allied advance into the North German Plain. The Divisional Headquarters for the 1st Airborne Division, with the 1st Air landing Brigade and the Polish 1st Independent Parachute Brigade were to land at Nijmegen, 1st Parachute Brigade was to land at Arnhem, and 4th Parachute Brigade was to land at Grave. The operation was fully planned and ready for launching when consecutive days of poor weather and Montgomery's concerns over increasing levels of German resistance caused him to postpone the operation before cancelling it altogether on 10th September.

Operation Market-Garden

In mid September the relatively limited objectives of Operation Comet were replaced by an altogether more grand and ambitious plan to bypass the Siegfried Line by hooking around its northern end, allowing the Allies to cross the Rhine with large forces and trap the German Fifteenth Army between Arnhem and the North Sea.

There was little accord with regard to Operation Market-Garden in the ranks of the allied commanders and on 10th September Dempsey firmly expressed to Montgomery his severe reservations concerning this new operational plan. Dempsey championed an advance north-eastwards between the Reichswald forest and the Ruhr to Wesel which clearly had a number of merits. Montgomery however countered with the explanation that he had just received a signal from London that something urgently must be done to destroy the V-2 launch sites around the Hague which were being used to bombard London. It was mainly on this evidence that the decision was taken that Operation Market-Garden must proceed in any event.

Montgomery flew to Brussels on the afternoon of 10th September to meet Eisenhower. It was an acrimonious meeting and in a typically theatrical gesture Montgomery ripped a file of Eisenhower's messages to shreds in front of him and demanded the focus be placed on a concentrated northern thrust. Eisenhower was convinced that German forces in the north faced imminent collapse but he remained adamant that advance on a broad front was correct. Faced with the evidence of the continuing V2 menace Eisenhower consented to Operation Market-Garden. Eisenhower however committed to only "limited priority" concerning supplies as he also sought to continue to support his advance on a broad front.

The new plan of action consisted of two simultaneous operations namely Operation Market under which a carpet of airborne forces of Lieutenant General Lewis H. Brereton's First Allied Airborne Army to seize bridges and other terrain, under tactical command of I Airborne Corps under Lieutenant-General Frederick Browning, and Operation Garden under which ground forces of the Second Army would move rapidly north along Highway 69 transiting swiftly over the bridges which had been seized by the parachutists. This advance was to be spearheaded by XXX Corps under Lieutenant-General Brian Horrocks and would be supported on its left by XXII Corps.

Allied Intelligence Reports

No sooner had the decision to launch Operation Market-Garden been taken than a large number of reports about German troop movements began to reach Allied high command. These reports included details concerning the identity and location of German armoured formations. Station X at Bletchley Park monitored and decrypted German ULTRA intelligence reports and sent them to senior Allied commanders, unfortunately these reports only reached army headquarters level and were not passed down any lower. On 16th September ULTRA decrypts revealed the movement of the 9th SS and 10th SS Panzer division to Nijmegen and Arnhem, creating enough concern for Eisenhower to send his Chief of Staff, Lieutenant General Walter Bedell Smith, to raise the issue with Montgomery. Montgomery dismissed Smith's concerns and refused to alter the plans for the landing of 1st Airborne Division at Arnhem.

Further information about the location of the German Panzer Divisions at Arnhem was revealed by aerial photographs of Arnhem taken by an RAF reconnaissance flight, as well as information from members of the Dutch resistance. Fearing that 1st Airborne Division might be in grave danger if it landed at Arnhem, the chief intelligence officer of the division, Major Brian Urquhart, arranged a meeting with Browning and informed him of the armour present at Arnhem. Browning dismissed his claims and ordered the division's senior medical officer to send Urquhart on sick leave on account of 'nervous strain and exhaustion.'

It is salutary to note that despite the stronger than expected

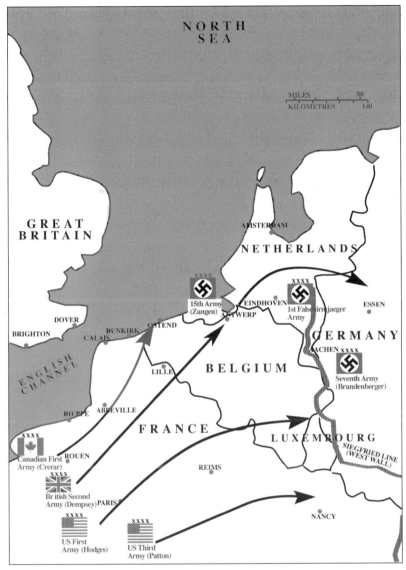

Montgomery's plan for Operation Market-Garden and beyond.

German forces on the ground, Operation Market employed only four of the six divisions of the First Allied Airborne Army. The U.S. 101st Airborne Division, under Major General Maxwell D. Taylor, would drop in two locations just north of XXX Corps start line and was ordered to take the bridges northwest of Eindhoven at Son and Veghel. The 82nd Airborne Division, under Brigadier General James M. Gavin, would drop northeast and further into German held territory in order to take the bridges at Grave and Nijmegen. The British 1st Airborne Division, under Major-General Roy Urquhart, with the Polish 1st Independent Parachute Brigade, under Brigadier General Stanis Law Sosabowski, drew the short straw and got the toughest assignment of all. They were ordered to drop at the extreme north end of the route and were tasked with capturing the road bridge at Arnhem and the rail bridge at Oosterbeek. It was envisaged that the 52nd (Lowland) Infantry Division would be flown to Deelen Airfield on D+5. 1st Airborne were also expected to have seized that objective.

It soon became obvious that Operation Market would be the largest airborne operation in history, delivering over 34,600 men of the 101st, 82nd and 1st Airborne Divisions and the Polish Brigade. 14,589 troops were landed by glider and 20,011 by parachute. Gliders also brought in 1,736 vehicles and 263 artillery pieces. 3,342 tons of ammunition and other supplies were brought by glider and parachute drop. Planning for Operation Market was compressed into an amazingly short period of time. After only six days, preparations were declared complete. The planning and training for the airborne drops at Sicily and Normandy had taken months. One United States Air Force historian noted that Market was the only large airborne operation of World War II in which the USAAF "had no training program, no rehearsals, almost no exercises, and a...low level of tactical training." Gavin, commanding the U.S. 82nd Airborne Division, was sceptical of the plan. In his diary he wrote, "It looks very rough. If I get through this one I will be very lucky."

In order to deliver this assemblage of 36 battalions of airborne infantry and their support troops to the continent, the First Allied Airborne Army had under its operational control the 14 groups of IX Troop Carrier Command, after 11th September the 16 squadrons of 38 Group (an organization of converted bombers providing support to resistance groups) and a transport formation, 46 Group. The combined force had 1,438 C-47/Dakota transports of which 1,274 came from USAAF and 164 were RAF. There were also a further 321 RAF bombers which had been converted into the transport role. The Allied glider force had been rebuilt in an amazingly short time after Normandy. By 16th September it could muster 2,160 CG-4A Waco gliders, plus 916 Airspeed Horsas and 64 General Aircraft Hamilcars. Glider pilots were in very short supply and as the U.S. could scrape together only 2,060 gliders it was decided that in order to maximise the forces available on the ground, none of its gliders would have a co-pilot but would instead carry an extra soldier as a passenger.

Eisenhower undertook to Montgomery that allied aircraft and American trucks would deliver 1,000 tons of supplies per day. In Montgomery's view this was far from adequate and Montgomery complained vociferously but vainly about this to the Vice-Chief of the Imperial General Staff in London, Lieutenant-General Sir Archibald Nye. To compound Montgomery's frustration it was decided that for Operation Market-Garden, the U.S. 82nd and 101st Airborne Divisions would be maintained from British stocks for all common items such as food and fuel. Non-common items like ammunition, ordnance and signal and engineer stores were delivered by the Red Ball Express or by rail to No. 6 Army Roadhead at Grammont. Three newly-arrived U.S. infantry divisions (the 26th, 95th, and 104th) were stripped of their transport, which was used to form provisional truck companies. These were assigned to the Red Ball Express, releasing eight companies to Red Lion, a special route to support Market-Garden. Red Lion convoys exceeded their target, delivering 650 tons per day instead of 500. Half of the tonnage hauled was supplies for the 82nd and 101st Airborne Divisions.

One other grave cause for concern was the fact that the 1400

Dakotas were expected to serve as both paratrooper transports and glider tugs. As IX Troop Carrier Command was called upon to provide all of the transports for both British parachute brigades, it was an insurmountable fact that even this massive force could deliver only 60% of the ground forces in one lift. This crucial factor was the reason for the fateful decision to split the troop lift schedule into successive days.

After much discussion it was decided ninety percent of the USAAF transports on the first day would drop parachute troops, with the same proportion coming back next day towing gliders on D+2. The split nature of the drop was to have far reaching consequences for the entire operation.

The Major Obstacles

Highway 69 (later nicknamed "Hell's Highway") was the road chosen as the planned route for Montgomery's narrow ground thrust codenamed Operation Garden. In 1944 the highway was two lanes wide and was generally raised on an embankment to sit above the surrounding flat terrain. One ominous factor which was not lost on the allied planners was the knowledge that the ground on either side of the highway was in most places far too soft and waterlogged to support tactical vehicle movement. There were also large number of dykes and countless drainage ditches. Dykes tended to be topped by trees or large bushes and roads and paths were almost invariably lined with trees which at that time of year were still in full leaf. This caused serious observation problems in the battle as it frequently limited lines of direct sight.

There were six major water obstacles between the XXX Corps' jumping-off point and the objective of the north bank of the Nederrijn. It was obvious that if the bridges could not be captured intact then the engineers would be faced with severe difficulties. The first obstacle facing XXX Corps was the Wilhelmina Canal at Son which was some 30 yards wide. Next was the Zuid-Willems

Canal at Veghel which was around 25 yards wide. The next obstacle was far more substantial and took the form of the Maas River at Grave was approximately 250 yards wide at the point at which the allies hoped to cross. Following on from that obstacle was the Maas-Waal Canal which was estimated to be 80 yards wide, then came the Waal River at Nijmegen which again was some 250 yards wide and finally the Nederrijn at Arnhem which was also around 80 yards wide.

The strong possibility existed that some, or even all, of these bridges could be demolished by the retreating Germans. Bridging a span of 250 yards is at the very limits of what could reasonably be achieved with the equipment available and the timescales allowed for Operation Market-Garden. Plans were therefore laid which demanded the seizure of the bridges across all these obstacles simultaneously — any failure to do so would result in serious delay at best or total disaster at worst. In preparation for the worst possible eventuality XXX Corps therefore had to have extensive contingency plans to rebuild all of the bridges which necessitated the assembly of a vast quantity of bridging material along with 2,300 vehicles to carry it all in and a force of 9,000 engineers to assemble the bridges if required.

As one might expect the area chosen for the operation was generally flat and open. Ironically for an operation taking place in Holland there were two strategically important hills to consider - both were substantial at over 300 feet high and in fact represented some of the highest ground in the Netherlands. The first hill lay north-west of Arnhem in the British sector. In the 82nd Airborne Division's zone, lay Groesbeek ridge. Seizure and defence of this feature was considered vital to holding the highway bridges.

Operational Considerations

The risk of Luftwaffe interception was correctly judged to be very small, but there were serious grounds for concern over the increasing number of flak units in the Netherlands, especially around Arnhem. Brereton's experience with tactical air operations allowed him to form the correct judgment that flak suppression would be sufficient to permit the troop carriers to operate without prohibitive loss. The invasion of Southern France had demonstrated that large scale daylight airborne operations were feasible. Daylight operations, in contrast to those in Sicily and Normandy, would have much greater navigational accuracy and time-compression of succeeding waves of aircraft, tripling the number of troops that could be delivered per hour. The time required to assemble airborne units on the drop zone after landing would be reduced by two-thirds.

IX Troop Carrier Command's transport aircraft had to tow gliders and drop paratroopers, duties that could not be performed simultaneously. Although every division commander requested two drops on the first day, Brereton's staff scheduled only one lift based on the need to prepare for the first drop by bombarding German flak positions for half a day and a weather forecast on the afternoon of 16th September, later proved to be incorrect, that the area would have clear conditions for four days, thus allowing subsequent drops on consecutive days. The forces marked for Operation Garden consisted primarily of XXX Corps and was initially spearheaded by the Guards Armoured Division, with the 43rd Wessex and 50th Northumbrian Infantry Divisions in reserve. They were expected to arrive at the south end of the 101st Airborne Division's area on D+1, the 82nd's by D+2 and the British 1st Airborne by D+4 at the very latest. The plan was that the airborne divisions would then join XXX Corps in the breakout from the Arnhem bridgehead which would take place on D+5.

The allies were aware that up to four days was a comparatively long time for a relatively weak airborne force to be expected to fight unsupported by heavy weapons or armoured forces. In addition the Allied paratroopers lacked adequate anti-tank weapons so a strong enemy armoured force appearing on the battlefield would pose an insurmountable problem. Unfortunately this was soon proved to be the case.

Given the high possibility of failure, Operation Market Garden was sanctioned purely on the grounds that to the best of the intelligence available it appeared to the Allied high command that the backbone of German resistance had broken. Most of the German Fifteenth Army in the area appeared to be fleeing from the Canadians and they were known to have no armour available. It was anticipated that XXX Corps would face limited resistance on their route up Highway 69 as the German defenders would be engaged in trying to contain the carpet of airborne forces which were dropped into their rear area.

The German Forces

As the German armies retreated towards the German frontier, they were constantly harried by air attacks and bombing raids by aircraft of the Royal Air Force and United States Army Air Force. These attacks inflicted many further casualties and destroyed yet more precious vehicles. Attempts to halt the Allied advance often seemed forlorn as hurried counter-attacks and blocking positions were brushed aside. The genuine rout of the Wehrmacht during July and August 1944 had led the Allies to believe that the German army was a spent force unable to reconstitute its shattered units. During those two months the Wehrmacht had suffered a string of defeats with heavy losses. Between 6th June and 14th August the Germans had suffered 300,000 casualties. Many of the formations which the Wehrmacht had possessed at the beginning of the Normandy campaign had been annihilated or had been reduced to skeleton formations by the end of August.

It is forgivable that the Allied High Command had formed the conclusion that the German forces had been routed. In doing so however they committed the cardinal sin of underestimating

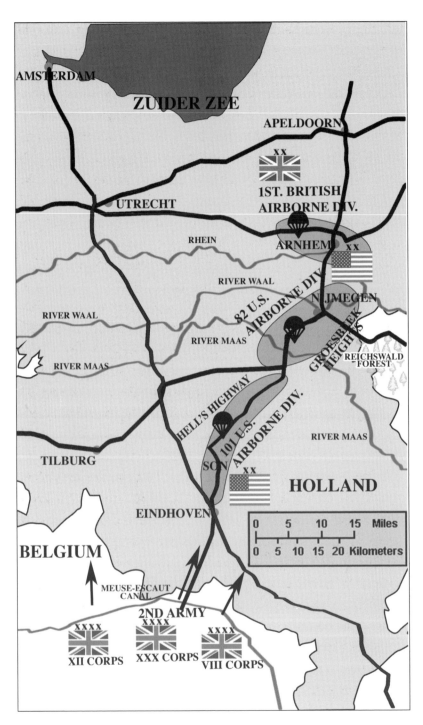

Operation Market-Garden

their enemy. The forces on the ground were shattered but the German Staff Planners were still a formidable opponent and they were able to conjure up some order from the chaos. By early September as a result of herculean efforts by the German Staff officers in the west the chaotic situation was beginning to show the first signs of order. The failure of the 21st Army Group to seal off the escape routes from the Scheldt Estuary area had allowed the 65,000 troops of the German Fifteenth Army to be extricated from the area they brought with them 225 guns and 750 trucks via a flotilla of commandeered freighters, barges and small boats.

Hitler also took a hand in proceedings and recalled Generalfeldmarschall Gerd von Rundstedt as Wehrmacht Commander-in-Chief West on July 2, and reinstated him in his old command. General Walter Model was demoted to command of Army Group B but this capable soldier still had a part to play in the battle. Rundstedt and Model immediately began to plan a defence with their force which was equivalent to around 13 divisions against, what the Wehrmacht intelligence indicated, were 50 Allied divisions which were about to be thrown against the German defence lines.

Walter Model was ordered by Rundstedt to stop the Allied advance. His first step was to order the 719th Infantry Division south to hold the line of the Albert Canal. Model next requested reinforcements from Germany, stating rather hopefully that he would require twenty-five infantry divisions and six armoured divisions to hold his lines. Meanwhile, Colonel General Kurt Student, commander of the Fallschirmjaeger (the German airborne forces) received orders from Alfred Jodl, Chief of the Operations Staff of the Oberkommando der Wehrmacht to immediately move from Berlin and proceed to the Netherlands, where he would collect all available units and build a front near the Albert Canal, which was to be held at all costs. This front was to be held by the newly designated First Falschirmjaeger or Parachute Army, an optimistic name for a formation which in reality consisted of units scattered throughout Germany and the Netherlands most of which were either in the process of being formed or being rebuilt from shattered remnants of existing formations.

Although the situation in August seemed dire beyond all prospect of redemption, under the guidance of men like Model and Student some kind of a cohesive German front was in fact beginning to form. Strong leadership, individual initiative and a good staff system was just about able to create a defensive line out of chaos. Despite all the pressure, things were beginning to work again on the ground for the Germans. On 4th September, as ordered, the 719th infantry division began to dig in along the Albert Canal and was unexpectedly joined by forces under the command of Lieutenant General Kurt Chill. Although Chill only officially commanded the battered remnants of the 85th Infantry Division which had suffered heavy casualties during the retreat from Normandy, he was an inspired soldier and had assumed command of the remnants of the 84th and 89th Infantry Divisions en route.

Although he had been ordered to take his shattered command to the Rhineland for rest and reinforcements, Chill considered he was entitled to act on his own initiative. Consequently he disregarded the easy option and instead moved his forces to the Albert Canal there he linked up with the 719th, his force providing an unexpected but very welcome influx of strength for the defenders. Chill also showed initiative in establishing 'reception centres' at all of the bridges crossing the Albert Canal. Small groups of retreating German soldiers were picked up, fed, re-equipped and turned into 'ad hoc' units known as Kampfgruppe.

By 7th September the 176th Infantry Division (a Kranken division composed of elderly men and men with various medical complaints) had also arrived from their defensive positions on the Siegfried Line. It was around this time too that the first elements of the putative First Parachute Army began to appear. At this stage the "Army" only consisted of approximately seven under strength Fallschirmjäger regiments amounting to around 20,000 airborne troops, along with a motley collection of anti-aircraft batteries and a mix of a mere 25 self-propelled guns and tank destroyers. In reality it was not even equivalent to the strength of a 1940 Panzer Division.

Kriegsmarine and SS units were also allocated to bolster Student's command. In respect of Model's desperate pleas for more armoured formations Hitler himself had promised that 200 of the latest Panther tanks would be sent straight from the production lines; he also ordered all Tiger tanks, Jagdpanther self-propelled guns and 88 mm guns that were available as reinforcements from Germany be immediately transferred to the West.

On 5th September, Model's forces were bolstered by the unheralded arrival of the II SS Panzer Corps. This force consisted of two Panzer Divisions, the 9th SS Hohenstaufen and 10th SS Frundsberg. The two Panzer divisions were under the command of SS-Obergruppenführer und General der Waffen-SS Wilhelm Bittrich, who had formerly commanded Hohenstaufen. The II SS Panzer Corps had been reduced to approximately 6,000-7,000 men, some 20-30% of its original strength. The Corps had been in continuous action since late June when it had first tangled with the British 21st Army around Caen. The Corps had also fought at Falaise where they had successfully maintained an escape route along which trapped German units had managed to escape from the destruction at the Faliase cauldron.

The escape into Holland had claimed yet more men and vehicles, and losses in officers and NCOs had been especially high so that the units were a mere shadow of their former selves. The II SS Corps had formerly consisted of three divisions but in a typical slight of hand by Hitler, the third division was

Hitler personally ordered all current production of the Panther tank to be rushed to support the forces in the west. It was vehicles such as these which made Frost's task all but impossible.

withdrawn from the order of battle but the title of Corps was retained by the much weaker force.

However, the core of the II SS Panzer Corps consisted of battle hardened survivors and with the first of the new Panther tanks already on their way, Model had the semblance of an armoured reserve at his disposal and therefore ordered the two divisions to begin the rest and refit process in what were considered to be safe areas behind the new German line. These areas coincidentally were to be Eindhoven for Hohenstaufen and Arnhem for Frundsberg. The 10th SS Panzer Division Frundsberg was to be quickly restored to full strength in order to provide an immediate armoured reserve. In the light of this, 9th SS Hohenstaufen Panzer Division was ordered to transfer all of its serviceable heavy equipment to its sister division; it was intended that the 9th would then be transported to Germany for replenishment.

At the time of Operation Market-Garden, 10th SS Panzer

Division Frundsberg had an approximate strength of 3,000 men; on paper the Division also boasted an armoured infantry regiment, divisional reconnaissance battalion, two artillery battalions and an engineer battalion, all partially motorized.

Other formations were appearing to strengthen the German defences. Between 16th September and 17th September two infantry divisions from Fifteenth Army assembled in Brabant, they too were massively under-strength but well-equipped and able to act as a reserve. Near Eindhoven and Arnhem a number of scratch formations were being assembled. Several SS units, including an NCO training battalion and a Panzergrenadier reserve battalion, were being prepared to enter combat and Luftwaffe and Kriegsmarine personnel were being grouped into Fliegerhorst and Schiffstammabteilung formations. There were also a number of training battalions that were being equipped, several depot battalions from the Hermann Goering Panzer Division and various artillery, anti-aircraft and field police units scattered throughout northern Holland.

German Intelligence

Von Rundstedt and Model expected a big Allied offensive to be imminent due to the large number of intelligence reports they were receiving that referred to a 'constant stream' of reinforcements being allocated to the right wing of the British Second Army. The senior intelligence officer of Army Group B believed that the Second Army would launch an offensive in the direction of Nijmegen, Arnhem and Wesel with its primary objective to reach the industrial area along the Ruhr river. He was convinced that airborne troops would be used in this offensive but was unsure as to where they would be deployed; suspecting areas of the Siegfried Line, north of Aachen or possibly even near the Saar.

The Course Of The Battle

DAY 1: SUNDAY, SEPTEMBER 17, 1944

The US 101st Battalion

Operation Market Garden opened with Allied success. In the first landing, almost all troops arrived on top of their drop zones without incident. In the 82nd Airborne Division, 89% of troops landed on or within 1,000 yards of their drop zones and 84% of gliders landed on or within 1,000 yards of their landing zones. This contrasted with previous operations where night drops had resulted in units being scattered by up to 12 miles. Losses to enemy aircraft and flak were light; German flak was described in reports as "heavy but inaccurate".

In the south, the US 101st met little resistance and captured four of five bridges. Crucially the bridge at Son was blown up as the US paratroops approached, after being delayed by a short engagement with a German Flak 88mm Anti-aircraft gun and a machine gun post. Later that day several small attacks by the German 59th Infantry Division were beaten off and small units of the 101st moved south of Son.

The US 82nd Battalion

To their north the US 82nd arrived and the small group dropped near Grave took the bridge in a rush. They also succeeded in capturing one of the vitally important bridges over the Maas-Waal canal, the lock-bridge at Heumen. The main effort of the 82nd was to seize the Groesbeek Heights and set up a blocking position there to prevent a German attack out of the nearby Reichswald and to deny the heights to German artillery observers. Gavin and Browning felt this must be the Division's priority. The 508th Parachute Infantry Regiment was tasked with taking the Nijmegen highway bridge. However this force did not start towards its objective until very late in the day. Had they attacked earlier they would have faced only a dozen German defenders. By the time the 508th finally got themselves into a position to attack, additional troops of the 9th SS Reconnaissance Battalion were arriving. The American attack failed, leaving the vital Nijmegen bridge in German hands. This was a desperate set back which jeopardised the success of the whole operation. Unlike some of the bridges to the south which were over smaller rivers and canals that could be bridged by engineering units, the Nijmegen and Arnhem bridges crossed two arms of the Rhine that could not be bridged easily. If either of the Nijmegen or Arnhem bridges were not captured and held, the advance of XXX Corps would be blocked and Operation Market Garden would be doomed to failure.

The 1st Airborne Division
The British 1st Airborne Division landed without serious incident but problems associated with the poor planning began to become apparent soon after the landings. Only half of the Division had arrived with the First Lift. Of these troops, only the three battalions of the 1st Parachute Brigade could be spared to actually advance upon the bridge. The remaining troops amounting to around half of the available manpower, had to remain behind to defend the drop zones overnight in anticipation of the arrival of the Second Lift on the following day. The Division's primary objective had therefore to be tackled by a force equivalent to less than half a division.

While the paratroopers formed up and marched the nine miles eastwards to Arnhem, the plan for Reconnaissance Squadron under Major Gough was to race to the bridge in their jeeps and motorcycles and seize it in a sudden coup de main and hold it until the rest of the Brigade arrived. The recce unit formed up and set off to the bridge late but having travelled only a short distance the vanguard was halted by a strong German defensive position and the squadron could make no further progress. This had grave consequences. Five hours after the initial landing, feeling that the British were tied down in Arnhem, the

Reconnaissance Battalion of the 9th Waffen-SS Panzer Division was able to cross the Arnhem bridge and drive to Nijmegen and assist in securing the bridge over the Waal branch of the Rhine.

The far reaching decision had been taken to split the approach of First Parachute Brigade into three columns each approaching the bridge by a different route. In this way two of the three battalions of the 1st Parachute Brigade were slowed down by small German units including elements of a training battalion which had been rushed into action and somehow managed to establish a thin blocking line which effectively blocked the most obvious routes into Arnhem. Gradually reinforcements from the 9th SS Panzer Division arrived and the German defences grew stronger and more determined.

The only exception to the universal pattern of failure was of course Lieutenant-Colonel John Frost's 2nd Battalion which had advanced eastwards along the southernmost road into Arnhem following the line of the river Rhine and gratefully found this route to the bridge largely undefended. Frost and his men arrived at the bridge towards evening of the 17th and quickly set up defensive positions at the north end of the bridge. Frost immediately made two full blooded attempts to dislodge the German defenders at the southern end of the arched steel bridge. Both attempts were beaten back with heavy losses.

The other battalions of the 1st Parachute Brigade continued to fare badly. The 3rd Battalion had only covered half the distance along the Utrechseweg to the bridge when they halted for the night and formed a defensive perimeter. The reason given was that darkness was falling and the rear of their column was still under heavy attack from units of an SS Panzer Grenadier battalion commanded by Sepp Krafft. In consequence it was felt that the thrust into Arnhem would stand a better chance of success in daylight.

The 1st Battalion moving along the Amsterdamseweg was similarly frustrated, yet continued the attempt to fight its way

The decision to drop the British paratroops nine miles from the bridge led to long delays while the troops, most of whom were on foot, formed up and marched off towards their objective.

through to the bridge. Throughout the night both battalions probed the defenders in an effort to find a way around the flank of the German line but despite frequent skirmishes they were completely unable to make any more progress towards the bridge.

Communication Breakdown

It was now that the consequence of poor planning again reared its ugly head. Some loss of communication between the bridge and Divisional Headquarters in one of the drop zones had been

A superb aerial photograph which gives a clear indication of the huge scale of Operation Market.

anticipated. This was not surprising as the Drop Zone was some 9 miles from the bridge and astonishingly the main radio used throughout the Division was the Type 22 set which was designed to have an effective range of just 3 miles. In fact it soon became obvious that the British radios did not function at any range whatsoever; some had difficulty receiving signals from just a few hundred meters and others received nothing at all. It was found after landing that the radios had been set to different frequencies, two of which coincided with those of German and British public broadcasting stations. Other theories have been advanced to explain the greatly reduced range of the 1st Airborne Division's radio sets. Subsequent tests using Type 22 sets have suggested that large deposits of iron in the soil could have been to blame. It is also possible that repeated operational stand-bys and cancellations (over a dozen drops were planned and then cancelled in the weeks prior to the operation) had led to sloppy battery charging procedures and lax supervision of this task. In any event, communication between 1st Airborne units was poor or non-existent while German defences were increasingly well coordinated and were now being constantly reinforced.

The only means for the British of calling for close air support was through two special American units dropped with the 1st Airborne Division. These units were equipped with "Veeps": jeeps having Very High Frequency SCR-193 crystal sets. It was found impossible to communicate with aircraft on the higher of two frequencies for this and to add to the frustration it was discovered that the sets could not be tuned to the lower frequency. Efforts were made to re-tune them, however the sets were rendered worthless as the Jeeps were soon destroyed by mortar fire. This event destroyed the 1st Airborne's only possible link with RAF fighter-bombers and robbed the 1st Airborne of their ace in the pack. The RAF pilots were under orders not to attack on their own initiative since from the air there was no easy way to distinguish friend from foe; together with poor weather, this led to a critical lack of air support.

XXX Corps Advance

On the morning of 17th September Lieutenant-General Brian Horrocks was given confirmation that the operation was to take place that very day. At 1230 hours Horrocks received a signal that the first wave of the airborne forces had actually left their bases within the United Kingdom and set the time for the ground attack to start at 1435 hours. At 1415 hours 300 guns of the Corps artillery opened fire, firing a rolling barrage in front of XXX Corps start line in a carpet of high explosive that was 1 mile wide and 5 miles in depth. The barrage was supported by seven squadrons of RAF Hawker Typhoons firing rockets at all known German positions along the road to Valkenswaard. The advance was led by tanks and infantry of the Irish Guards. The advance started on time when Lieutenant Keith Heathcote, commanding the lead tank, ordered his driver to advance. The lead units of the Irish Guards Group had broken out of XXX Corps bridgehead on the Meuse-Escaut canal and crossed into the Netherlands by 1500 hours. Shortly after crossing the border however the Irish Guards were ambushed by infantry and anti-tank guns dug in on both sides of the main road.

Communication was much easier as regards the Operation Garden part of the battle and as the forces were still relatively close to their start line the artillery were able to redouble their efforts and as fresh waves of Hawker Typhoons were called in, the Irish Guardsmen once again moved forward to clear the German positions. From prisoner interrogations it was soon discovered that these positions were manned by elements from two German parachute battalions and two battalions of the 9th SS Division. This was the first indication that the German defenders were clearly capable of mounting a far more serious defence than had originally been anticipated. Nonetheless the Irish Guards soon overcame the initial German forces flanking the road. Further interrogation of captured German soldiers led to some of them willingly pointing out the remaining German positions. The fighting soon died down and the advance resumed. By last light of 17th September the town of Valkenswaard had been reached and occupied by the Irish Guards Group.

Horrocks had expected the Irish Guards to advance the full 13 miles to Eindhoven within two-three hours, however the fierce resistance encountered meant that they had only covered 7 miles. The operation was already starting to fall behind schedule. In Valkenswaard, engineers were moved up to construct a 60 yard Class 40 Bailey bridge over a stream; this heavy task was completed within 12 hours.

German Counter Measures

From the German perspective the allied plan of campaign was

soon all too clear. Field Marshal Walter Model was billeted at the Totenberg Hotel in Oosterbeek, a village to the west of Arnhem, when the British 1st Parachute Brigade began to land in the countryside to the west of Oosterbeek. Initially he concluded that the allied forces were commandos attempting to kidnap him. Model therefore made a rush for a safer location. Meanwhile, Wilhelm Bittrich, commanding the II SS Panzer Corps, had no such fanciful notions and kept a much clearer head. He immediately sent a reconnaissance company of the 9th SS Panzer Division to Nijmegen to reinforce the bridge defences. By midnight, however, Model had also gained an overall impression of the situation and issued orders that proved immensely beneficial to the defence of Arnhem. The surprise and confusion usually associated with efforts to defend against airborne operations was therefore absent at Arnhem and the advantage of surprise was further reduced by the decision to land so far from the objective. As a result of the quick reactions of the German commanders, the questionable decision to land on a drop zone nine miles away from the prime objective already appeared to represent a glaring mistake.

D+1: MONDAY, SEPTEMBER 18

For the morning of 18th September Allied weather forecasters correctly predicted that England would be blanketed under a layer of fog. The Second Lift was therefore postponed for a crucial three hours. In that time thick low clouds began to develop over the southern part of the battle zone, spreading during the day over the area, hampering supply and air support. Bad weather was destined to blight the entire operation. Seven of the next eight days saw poor weather conditions which were so bad that all air operations had to be cancelled altogether on September 22 and September 24.

The 1st and 3rd Parachute Battalions continued their efforts to push on towards the Arnhem bridge. During the early hours of 18th September they actually made good progress but they were halted by increasingly effective German resistance as soon as it became light. With their long and unwieldy columns the paratroops were not in the best fighting formation and were frequently having to halt to beat off what were seemingly random attacks at all points. The German forces soon had the upper hand and isolated elements of the two battalions were fought to a standstill and captured.

Early in the morning of the 18th the small Kampfgruppe of the 9th SS Reconnaissance Battalion SS-Hauptsturmfuhrer Graubner which had been sent south by Bittrich the day before, concluded it was not needed in Nijmegen. Graubner decided therefore to return to Arnhem where his force which included half tracks and armoured cars might prove to be of more value. Although he was well aware of the British troops at the northern end of the bridge, SS-Hauptsturmfuhrer Graubner attempted to cross by force. From the course of the famous action which followed it was soon apparent that it was not just the British who were capable of underestimating the forces ranged against them. Frost's men put up a ferocious resistance and helter skelter dash by armoured cars, half tracks and lorried infantry was beaten back with heavy losses including its commanding officer, SS-Hauptsturmfuhrer Graubner.

By the end of the day the 1st and 3rd Parachute Battalions had actually entered Arnhem and were now within just 1 mile of the bridge. However they had taken heavy casualties and were now reduced to approximately 200 men, one-sixth their original strength. Most of the officers and non-commissioned officers had been killed, wounded or captured. The Paras now badly needed reinforcement but Second Lift was delayed by fog and jumped onto a landing zone under heavy attack but nonetheless landed at something like full strength. The second wave consisted of the 4th Parachute Brigade consisting of the 10th, 11th and 156th Battalions of the Parachute Regiment, commanded by Brigadier-General John Winthrop Hackett and C and D Companies of the 2nd South Staffordshire Regiment.

D+1 The US 82nd Airborne

The situation confronting the US 82nd Airborne on D+1 was also beginning to deteriorate. Grave proved to be well defended and German forces continued to press hard on the perimeter of 82nd troops deployed on the Groesbeek heights to the east of Nijmegen. The 505th Parachute Infantry Regiment defended against German attacks in Horst, Grafwegen and Riethorst. Early in the day, German counterattacks seized one of the Allied landing zones where the Second Lift was scheduled to arrive at 13:00. However, the 508th Parachute Infantry Regiment launched a counter attack at 13:10 and cleared the landing zone by 14:00, capturing 16 German flak pieces and 149 prisoners. Fortunately the second lift had been delayed by bad weather in Britain and did not actually arrive until 15:30 otherwise they would have been dropping into German territory. This lift brought in elements of the 319th and 320th Glider Field Artillery battalions, the 456th Parachute Field Artillery battalion and medical support elements. Twenty minutes later, 135 B-24 bombers dropped supplies from low level, 80% of these were recovered.

D+1 US 101st Airborne zone

In the wake of the loss of the bridge at Son, the 101st unsuccessfully attempted to capture a similar bridge a few kilometres away at Best but found the approach blocked. Other units continued moving to the south and eventually reached the northern end of Eindhoven.

D+1 XXX Corps

The Irish Guards Group resumed the Operation Garden offensive and began to advance once more. They soon found themselves facing determined resistance from German infantry and tanks. Nonetheless the attack was pressed home and around noon, elements of 101st Airborne were met by the lead reconnaissance units from XXX Corps. Bad news soon followed however as at 16:00 radio contact alerted the main force that the Son bridge had been destroyed and requested that a bailey bridge be brought forward. By nightfall the Guards Armoured Division had established itself in the Eindhoven area, however transport columns were jammed in the packed streets of the town and suffered heavy losses to both men and vehicles as a result of a heavy German aerial bombardment during the night. XXX Corps engineers, supported by German prisoners of war, constructed a class 40 bailey bridge within 10 hours across the Wilhelmina Canal.

During the day the British VIII and XII Corps, supporting the main attack, had forged bridgeheads across Meuse-Escaut Canal while facing stiff German resistance; 50th (Northumbrian) Infantry Division was transferred from XXX Corps to VIII Corps so to relieve XXX Corps from the task of securing the ground gained thus far. Throughout the day strong German attacks were launched against XXX Corps and against the newly gained bridgeheads over the Meuse-Escaut Canal, all without success.

D+2: TUESDAY, SEPTEMBER 19

During the early morning hours the 1st Parachute Brigade began its attack towards Arnhem Bridge, with the 1st Battalion leading, supported by remnants of the 3rd Battalion, with the 2nd South Staffordshire's on the 1st Battalion's left flank and the 11th Battalion following. As soon as it became light the 1st Battalion was spotted and halted by fire from the main German defensive line. Trapped in open ground and under heavy fire from three sides, the 1st Battalion disintegrated and what remained of the 3rd Battalion also fell back. The 2nd South Staffordshire's were similarly cut off and, save for about 150 men, were totally overwhelmed by midday. The 11th Battalion, which had stayed

The local Dutch resistance were soon in evidence. Local volunteers are seen here with the men of the US 82nd Airborne.

out of much of the fighting, was similarly overwhelmed by German forces as they had been in exposed positions while attempting to capture high ground to the north. With no hope of breaking through, the 500 remaining men of these four battalions withdrew westwards in the direction of the main force still located 3 miles away in Oosterbeek.

The 2nd Battalion and attached units now reduced to a force of approximately 600 men were still in control of the northern approach ramp to the Arnhem bridge. The Germans recognised that they could not be moved by infantry attacks or by a rush of vehicles such as those that had been bloodily repulsed on the previous day. The Germans therefore resorted to the use of almost point blank artillery and heavily shelled the short British perimeter. Everything available in the German armoury was now thrown into the battle including mortars, artillery and tanks. The German tactic was to systematically demolish each house in order to enable their infantry to exploit gaps and dislodge the defenders. The attackers had all too quickly become desperate defenders but they continued to wage a fierce battle against enormous odds and somehow the British clung to their positions and much of the perimeter was held.

To the north of Oosterbeek the 4th Parachute Brigade led another attempt by the 1st Airborne Division to break through the German lines and reach the bridge. A combination of communication difficulties and enemy resistance caused the attack to fail with heavy losses. The Division, now scattered far and wide and hard pressed by the enemy on all sides had lost its offensive capability. Unable to help Lt.-Col. Frost at the bridge, the remaining soldiers attempted to withdraw into a defensive pocket at Oosterbeek and hold a bridgehead on the north bank of the Rhine.

One unit which could have provided valuable support were the parachute elements of the Polish 1st Independent Parachute Brigade but they had remained in England because of dense fog. Their gliders, mainly carrying anti-tank guns and vehicles, were able to take off but had the misfortune to arrive above the landing zone just as the 4th Parachute Brigade was retreating across it and the gliders came under heavy fire from German units pursuing the Brigade.

D+2 The US 82nd Airborne

Early in the morning the 504th Parachute Infantry Regiment of the US 82nd Airborne Division made contact with XXX Corps at Grave. This enabled the Regiment to move on to other missions and place the 3rd Battalion in divisional reserve. By the morning of 19th September, the British Guards Armoured Division of XXX Corps had linked up with the main body of the US 82nd Airborne.

D+2 XXX Corps

According to the Operation Garden plan, XXX Corps should have been approaching Arnhem but they were still stuck eight miles away. Nonetheless they were still six hours ahead according to the timetable; the earlier delays had been made up by a valiant effort. A combined effort to take the Nijmegen bridge was mounted by two companies from the Guards Armoured Division and the 2nd Battalion, US 505th Parachute Infantry Regiment. The attack got within 400 yards of the bridge before being halted and although skirmishing continued throughout the night no further progress was made. A plan was made to attack the south end of the bridge again while the 3rd Battalion, 504th Parachute Infantry Regiment, planned to cross the river in boats a mile downstream and then attack the north end. The boats, requested for late afternoon didn't arrive. Once again XXX Corps was held up in front of a bridge which should

Vehicles of the Guards Armoured Division of the British XXX Corps
passing through Grave having linked up with 82nd US-Airborne Division.
17 - 20 September 1944

have been captured before they arrived.

The 1st and 5th battalions, Coldstream Guards, were attached to the division. However they were short of vital supplies. C47 planes were sent to supply the unit but they were unsuccessful; the supplies were dropped from a high altitude and could not be recovered. Bad weather over English bases prevented the scheduled supplies mission, ending any hope of reinforcements for the 82nd Airborne.

Just before 10 in the morning, the 504th Parachute Infantry Regiment moved forward to Wijchen, to attack the Edith bridge from its south end. After a fierce encounter the bridge was secured. They then advanced to a second bridge at the South of Wijchen, of which they also took control.

To the south of Wijchen towards Eindhoven Veghel, several units of the 101st Battalion, who had been sent to take Best the day before, were forced to retreat under intense pressure from the German artillery. The fighting became general and a confused pattern of attack and counter attack developed across the battlefield. British tanks arriving during the day helped push back the Germans by late afternoon. Nearby however a small force of Panther tanks arrived at Son and commenced firing on the Bailey bridge. However the Germans failed to make any gains, thanks to the newly installed anti-tank guns on the bridge the area was secured.

D+3: WEDNESDAY, SEPTEMBER 20

Lt. Colonel John Frost's force at Arnhem bridge continued to hold and established communication with the prospective reinforcements from 1st Division around noon. However Frost learned to his dismay that the reinforcements had been bogged down in fighting around Nijmegen and couldn't reach the bridge. By the afternoon the British positions around the north end of Arnhem bridge had weakened considerably. Casualties, mostly wounded, were high from constant shelling. A lack of ammunition especially anti-tank munitions, enabled enemy armour to approach British positions with impunity in order to demolish British positions using point-blank range. Food, water and medical supplies were scarce, and many buildings were on fire. Amazingly a two-hour truce was somehow arranged between the enemies to evacuate the wounded which now included Lieutenant-Colonel Frost himself. The men were taken into German captivity but it was preferable to almost certain death inside the bridgehead. Frederick Gough took over as commander when Frost was captured.

All along the perimeter the Germans gradually overcame individual pockets of British resistance throughout the day. Eventually they gained control of the northern entrance to the bridge which permitted German reinforcements to filter south in order to reinforce their own units fighting further south near Nijmegen. The remaining British troops continued to fight on, some with just fighting knives but by early Thursday morning almost all had been taken prisoner. The last radio message broadcast from the bridge - "Out of ammo, God save the King" - was heard only by German radio intercept operators.

The defence of the bridge has justifiably gone down in the annals of military history as a bold and inspired feat of arms. Originally it was estimated that the 1st Airborne Division, 10,000 strong, would only need to hold Arnhem bridge for two days. In reality a much smaller force of just 740 had held it for twice as long against far heavier opposition than anticipated. While 81 British soldiers died defending Arnhem bridge, German losses cannot be stated with any accuracy, they were believed to be very high; 11 units known to have participated in the fighting reported 50% casualties after the battle. In memory of the fighting there, the bridge was later renamed the "John Frost Bridge".

The remnants of the 1st Airborne Division were now gathering at Oosterbeek for their own last stand; those already there were not seriously challenged by the enemy throughout the day. To the east of the village the 1st, 3rd and 11th Parachute Battalions and 2nd South Staffordshire's were organised into a defensive position. There was fierce fighting throughout the afternoon, as the limited British forces withheld a fierce German attack trying to secure the Rhine.

In the woods to the west of Oosterbeek the 4th Parachute Brigade was fighting its way towards the divisional perimeter but was under severe attack from German troops supported by artillery, mortars and tanks. Their casualties were heavy; the 10th Battalion reached Oosterbeek in the early afternoon but with only 60 men.

Further in the rear, the 156th Parachute Battalion was being more hard pressed and was forced to fight off numerous enemy attacks before mounting counter-attacks of their own. The battalion, down to 150 men mounted a desperate bayonet charge to capture a hollow in the ground in the woods, in which they remained pinned by enemy attacks for the next eight hours. Towards the end of the day the 75 men who still could, broke through the German lines and retreated into the shrinking British pocket at Oosterbeek.

Little Omaha

The boats ordered by the 82nd Airborne the day before, failed to arrive until afternoon and a hasty daylight assault crossing was ordered. At about 3 in the afternoon the 3rd Battalion, 504th PIR accompanied by sappers from 615 Field Squadron and 11th Field Company Royal Engineers made the crossing in 26 canvas assault boats into well-defended positions. The American unit had no training on the British-made boats and a shortage of paddles required some soldiers to paddle the boats with their rifles. About half the boats survived the crossing under heavy fire. In another heroic incident the surviving Paras then assaulted across 200 meters of open ground on the far bank and seized the north end of the bridge. German forces withdrew from both ends of the bridge which was then rushed by Guards tanks and the 2nd Battalion, 505th PIR. The costly attack was nicknamed "Little Omaha" by the Americans in reference to the bloody episode on Omaha Beach. When Lieutenant-General Dempsey of the Second Army met Brigadier General Gavin, commander of the U.S. 82nd Airborne Division, he is reported to have said (in reference to the Nijmegen attack), "I am proud to meet the commander of the greatest Division in the world today."

To the east, German attacks on the heights made significant progress, capturing the only remaining bridge suitable for tanks. A counterattack at Mook by elements of the 505th PIR and 4th Battalion, the Coldstream Guards forced the Germans back from the bridge in the late evening. The 508th PIR lost ground at Im Thal and Legewald when attacked by German infantry and tanks. By now it was evident that the German plan was to cut off access to Highway 69 which would split up the Airborne units and cut off the advance elements of XXX Corps. To the south, running battles between the 101st and various German units continued. Eventually several Panther tanks managed to cut the main road but these had to be pulled back when they ran low on ammunition and the situation was stabilised.

D+4: THURSDAY, SEPTEMBER 21

Approximately 3,500 survivors of the 1st Airborne Division established themselves in the buildings and woods around Oosterbeek with the intention of holding a bridgehead on the north side of the Rhine until XXX Corps could arrive. Throughout the day their position was heavily attacked on all sides. In the southeast, Lonsdale Force (the remnants of the 1st, 3rd, and 11th Parachute Battalions and 2nd South Staffordshire's) fought off a large attack which was strongly supported by the fire of German light artillery. In the north the 7th King's Own Scottish Borderers were almost overrun by a superior German force, but a counterattack with bayonets restored the situation enabling the heavily depleted battalion to occupy a narrower front.

The most serious attack of the day was made at dawn against "B" Company, 1st Battalion, Border Regiment which controlled a vital area of high ground overlooking the Heveadorp ferry crossing at Driel. This was the Airborne division's only straightforward means of receiving reinforcements from the south. The company was attacked by enemy armour and infantry, using captured French tanks equipped with flamethrowers. The B Company were heavily outnumbered and the entire area was lost. Counter attacks failed and the remnants of the company were redeployed closer to the British forces at the bridge. The division was now left in a precarious position, controlling just 700 meters of the riverbank.

A supply attempt by RAF Stirlings was disrupted by the only significant Luftwaffe fighter intervention during the operation. German Fw 190s intercepted the Stirlings at low altitude and shot down 15 overall. Anti-aircraft fire accounted for 8 further losses. The Fw 190s were able to penetrate the screen of Allied fighters sent to cover the drop when the U.S. 56th Fighter Group was late in arriving in its patrol sector between Lochem and Deventer. The 56th redeemed itself to an extent by shooting down 15 of the 22 Fw 190s as they departed the scene of carnage.

After two days of delay due to the weather, the Polish 1st Independent Parachute Brigade under Major-General Stanislaw Sosabowski finally entered the battle on the afternoon of September 21. Two of the brigade's three battalions were dropped amidst heavy German fire, opposite the 1st Airborne Division's position on a new drop zone south of the Rhine near the village of Driel. Poor coordination by the RAF and persistent attacks by Luftwaffe aircraft caused their supplies to be dropped 15 km (9 miles) away on the opposite side of the Rhine.

Intending to use the Heveadorp ferry to reinforce the division, they discovered that the opposite bank was dominated by the enemy and that the ferry was missing; it was later found downstream past the road bridge in a totally unserviceable condition. Unable to help the trapped British forces, the Polish withdrew into a perimeter Driel for the night.

Despite the capture of Nijmegen bridge and the clearing of the town on the previous evening, the five tanks of the 82nd Guards Armoured Division which were across the river did not begin to advance until 18 hours later. Lieutenant-General Brian Horrocks along with Brigadier General Gavin claimed he needed this delay to sort out the confusion among his troops. This was a controversial decision that has been examined often in the years since. It would appear that the reason for the delay lay in the fact that the Coldstream Guards Group were repulsing an attack on the Groesbeek position, the Irish Guards Group had gone back to Eindhoven to meet another attack, the Grenadiers had just captured the approaches to the bridge with the US paratroops and the Welsh Guards were in 82nd Airborne reserve. The Guards Armoured Division was scattered over twenty-five square miles of the south bank of the Waal.

The Market Garden plan depended upon a single highway as the route of advance and supply. This imposed a delay since other units could not be deployed on other routes to maintain momentum. Brigadier General Gavin's diary comment was: "Had Ridgway been in command at that moment, we would have been ordered up that road in spite of all our difficulties, to save the men at Arnhem." He is silent on the 36 hour delay caused by his failure to capture the bridge on schedule.

Another version of events quotes Captain Lord Carrington " I certainly met an American officer the Airborne were all very glad to see us and get some support; no one suggested we should press on to Arnhem.". 'Let us be frank. The 82nd should have taken the Nijmegen bridge on D-Day, September 17. By failing to do so Gavin made a major contribution to the failure of the entire Arnhem operation and it will not do to pass the blame for that failure on to the British or to captain Lord Carrington.'

The delay at Nijmegan enabled the Germans to reinforce the defence already established at Ressen, south of Arnhem aided by use of the bridge following their capture of its northern end. The delayed advance of the 82ndGuards was soon halted by a firm German defensive line. The Guards did not have the strength to outflank it, the 43rd Division was ordered to take over the lead, work its way around the enemy positions and make contact with the Polish at Driel. The 43rd was 30km away and it was not until the following day that the whole division crossed the River Waal and began its advance.

The Germans, clearly starting to gain the upper hand, continued their counter-attacks all along the path of XXX Corps, although the Corps still managed to advance and the 101st Airborne Division continued to exploit its gains.

In the afternoon C-47 glider tugs and C-47 cargo carriers delivered supplies to the 82nd Airborne Division. About 60% of the supplies were recovered partly with the help of Dutch civilians. Most of the 82nd and 101st, reinforced with British armoured units, were engaged in defensive fighting with the objective of holding the highway corridor, which was extremely important in order to maintain a supply route.

After the victory of the 504th Parachute Infantry Regiment at Wijchen the Germans tried to attack the Edith bridge from the north end. The 504th Parachute Infantry Regiment requested help from the 101st Airborne Division. Ultimately the Germans were not strong enough to defend their position and had to abandon the bridges in Wijchen to the 504th Parachute Infantry Regiment.

D+5 FRIDAY, SEPTEMBER 22

The Germans, wary after unsuccessful and costly attacks the previous day, shelled and mortared the airborne positions heavily. By the end of the battle some 110 guns had been brought to Oosterbeek as the Germans shifted to the tactics that had worked so well at Arnhem bridge. Attacks were limited, conducted against specific positions and even individual houses. Numerous well-sited British anti-tank guns also caused German reluctance to attack. The survivors of the 1st Airborne were outnumbered 4 to 1. The Polish 1st Parachute Brigade at Driel, who were unable to cross the Rhine in the ferry's absence, nonetheless forced a redeployment of German forces. Fearing a Polish attempt to recapture Arnhem bridge the Germans withdrew 2,400 troops from Oosterbeek. They were moved south of the river to engage the Polish paratroopers at Driel, making attacks to little effect through the day.

The fog lifted as leading elements of the 43rd Division attempted to advance to Driel, exposing them to German fire. They arrived in Driel during the evening, trying to reach the Polish brigade who had been bogged down in the town. Lacking assault craft, an unsuccessful attempt was made that night to put elements of the Polish brigade across the river. British and Polish engineers on both sides of the Rhine had worked through the day to improvise a crossing using small boats linked by signals cable, but the cable kept breaking, forcing the Polish troops to slowly row across against the strong current. Only 52 men of the 8th Polish Parachute Company survived the crossing, made under heavy German fire, before a halt was called at dawn.

Despite the British controlling nearly all of the area, the Germans successfully managed to take control of a small area of road, preventing the British from further advancing towards Arnhem.

D+6: SATURDAY, SEPTEMBER 23

The Germans had figured out what the Poles were attempting to do and they spent the rest of the day trying to cut off the British from the riverside. The British managed to hold on to their

Fierce house to house fighting continued in Arnhem on D+1 and D+2
before the British forces were compelled to withdraw to Oosterbeek.

positions resulting in both sides suffering heavy losses. The Germans also attacked the Poles on the south side in order to tie them down. By this stage several tanks arrived from XXX Corps and they too were beaten off. Boats and engineers from the Canadian army also arrived that day and another river crossing that night landed 150 troops of the Polish 3rd Parachute Battalion on the north bank of the Rhine.

To the south several more German attacks from their position astride the road were stopped. XXX Corps then sent a unit of the Guards Armoured Division 19km south and re-took the road, taken the night before, from the German Army. The rest of the force to the north continued to wait for infantry to move up, still only a few kilometres south of Arnhem.

The 325th GIR was finally delivered to reinforce the 82nd Airborne, originally planned for September 19, 4 days earlier, they arrived far too late to affect the battle in that sector.

D+7: SUNDAY, SEPTEMBER 24

Another German force cut the road to the south of Veghel and set up defensive positions for the night. It was not clear to the Allies at this point how much of a danger this represented but the principal objective of Operation Market Garden, i.e. the Allied crossing of the Rhine, was abandoned this day and the decision made to go over to the defensive with a new front line in Nijmegen. Nonetheless, an attempt was made on Sunday night to reinforce the 1st Airborne Division with the 4th Battalion, The Dorsetshire Regiment. Two companies were put across the river but the location of the crossing point was ill-advised and the Dorset's landed among German positions. Fragmented by their landing and immediately pinned down, of the 315 men who crossed, only 75 reached Oosterbeek; the remainder were taken prisoner. As a result of this failure, it was decided to withdraw the 1st Airborne Division from its bridgehead on the northern side of the Rhine.

D+8: MONDAY, SEPTEMBER 25

At dawn, the 1st Airborne Division received their orders to withdraw across the Rhine; called Operation Berlin. This could not be done until nightfall and in the meantime the division struggled to survive. In a departure from their cautious attritional tactics of the previous days, the Germans formed two potent SS battle groups and made a significant advance along a narrow front in the eastern sector. The Germans successfully broke through the thin British line and the 1st Airborne Division were put under immense pressure. However the attack met with increasing resistance as it pushed deeper into the British lines and was finally broken up by a heavy bombardment of the 64th Medium Regiment.

Employing every ruse to give the Germans the impression that their positions were unchanged, the 1st Airborne Division began its withdrawal later that evening. British and Canadian engineer units ferried the troops across the Rhine, covered by the Polish 3rd Parachute Battalion on the north bank. By early the next morning they had withdrawn 2,398 survivors, leaving 300 men to surrender on the north bank at first light. All of the force could have escaped but the arrival of daylight exposed the deceit and the resulting German fire prevented the escape of the very last batch.

In the final analysis, out of approximately 10,600 men of the 1st Airborne Division and other units who fought north of the Rhine, 1,485 had died and 6,414 were taken prisoner. In terms of casualties suffered and objectives taken Operation Market, for the British forces at least, marked a major defeat.

To the south the newly-arrived 50th (Northumbrian) Infantry Division attacked the German forces holding the highway and secured it by the next day. This was the last significant action of Operation Market-Garden.

Allied positions in the Nijmegen Salient, as it came to be known, were manned throughout the rest of September and

October by the airborne units which had fought the battle before being handed over to the First Canadian Army in November 1944. The battle lines in the Arnhem area remained almost unchanged until February 1945, when Operation Veritable was launched on the Rhineland. The final axis of advance was east into Germany instead of north towards Arnhem.

CHAPTER 2

FROM NORMANDY TO HAMBURG

Extracts from the war diary of Captain Graham Davies. Royal Artillery 133 Field Regiment
53rd Welsh Infantry Division.
Xxii Corps British 21st Army.

In 1944 there were a great many unsung heroes quietly doing their bit for King and Country. Many of these men such as Captain Graham Davies were modest and unassuming men who nonetheless realised that they were playing a part in one of the great dramatic episodes of world history. Captain Davies and his battery of 133 Field Artillery formed part of the famous 53rd (Welsh) Infantry Division which as part of XXII Corps and later of XXX Corps took part in many of the most famous campaigns of 1944 including The Battle For Caen, The Falaise Pocket, Operation Garden, The Ardennes Offensive and the Rhine Crossings. We are fortunate that Capt Davies in his lifetime had the presence of mind to record a diary of his experiences. Like so many others, this fascinating historical document has lain unpublished for over 65 years and would have remained so had it not been brought to our attention by his son Gwilym, to whom we are indebted for permission to reproduce this extract.

This particular version of events is worthy of publication as it gives the reader a different perspective on the Arnhem battle from an often overlooked point of view. The story of the battle

Captain Graham Davies RA -1922-2005. Captain Davies saw action in most of the principal engagements of the war in the west.

which is usually told from the perspective of Operation Market, naturally relies upon the view from the very front lines. This memoir is rather different. This is the artillery man's tale and concerns the events of Operation Garden as they were witnessed by a Captain controlling a troop of 25 pounder field guns. This short extract should hopefully provide the reader with a new insight into the contribution made by the thousands of men who formed the supporting arms of the British 21st Army. We are sure that students of military history will welcome the opportunity to embrace a primary source document which throws new light on the battle from another angle.

"On 6th June 1944 we finally heard that the big day had arrived. The first wave of troops had actually landed in Normandy that morning. The British population had gone mad. It seemed that everyone had come out to see what was happening. Even in southern England they were cheering us like mad as if we had actually taken part in the landing itself.

People were thrusting refreshments at us – which we were

literally forced to accept. Never before or since have I consumed such a motley, ill-assorted mixture of foods. Fish paste, meat and jam sandwiches interspersed with little cakes, drinks of lemonade, tea and coffee, all consumed at double quick time in order to hand the container back to the kind donor who was running alongside.

We were completely confined to the camp at Epping Forest and were surrounded by high wire fencing. Looking through the wire one day I was amazed to see some friends from my old HAA Regiment 117 passing. A quick shout brought them over. They were now stationed just a few hundred yards away, part of the anti-aircraft defence of the City. We were held here for some time because of the bad weather in France. Eventually we were given the opportunity of having Communion, and then down to the East India docks, where we boarded our American Liberty ship, the USS William Phipps. The Captain seemed very young, with a well-trimmed Imperial beard. We set sail, and got well out into the estuary before we had to heave to and await orders. Apparently it was because of the continuing bad weather, which had created a massive build up in the reinforcements waiting to land.

Eventually our turn came and I think it was the morning of the 23rd of June that saw us land at Arromanches. The famous Mulberry Harbour did not yet exist, there were a couple of elements only in the bay. Our vehicles were being offloaded by crane to LCT's (Landing Craft Tanks) which were positioned alongside. We would have to scramble down large nets, which had been draped down the ship's side. Although things were pretty quiet, I know that we had a peculiar gut feeling, knowing that at long last we were actually landing in enemy held territory, and that we were about to put all our training into practice as we really came up against the enemy. As my truck, a fifteen hundredweight had been the last to be loaded on the ship, it was the first to be offloaded. I would be leading the charge! A couple of hundred yards away, a sister battery was going through the same motions. I was the Troop Leader of F Troop, which was the junior troop of the junior battery in the regiment. And I was its junior officer. My troop commander was Captain David Thompson, as good a man as you could ever wish to meet. We were all proud of our units, and always keen to accept a challenge. David had been able to assess the general situation and could see that it would be a close thing as to who would land first. He shouted to me, and my driver Gunner Bell, to get a move on. The LCT left the ship's side and headed for the shore. We were still quite a way out from the shore when we grounded, the front of the LCT dropped and old Bell gave her the works. We were actually in a few feet of water, but ploughed inshore rapidly to arrive first, to a loud cheer from those left on board the William Phipps.

We roared up the beach and were guided off by several beach-masters, then to an open area where we had to remove all our waterproofing. To drive too far with that on would seriously damage the engine. When we had all assembled and finished our de-waterproofing, we were led to action positions. There would be no great time to pass before we were to engage the enemy.

Perhaps I should digress a little here and explain how life in action would differ from that life we had become accustomed to in training. The active components of a battery become split. The OC (Officer Commanding) is a Major, and under him, he has two Troop Commanders who are Captains. These three people spend virtually all their time with their opposite numbers in the particular infantry units they are supporting. Each troop position of four guns is in charge of a subaltern (Lieutenant) called a GPO (Gun Position Officer). The GPO has as his assistant a TL (Troop Leader). The eight guns of the battery are synchronised by the CPO (Command Post Officer) who is the senior subaltern. So the infantry liaison team and the gun position team can now spend months apart, the only lines of communication being by radio or telephone. The troop commanders simply identify the target by one means or another and the gun teams are given the necessary information to respond. Each GPO is responsible for correctly locating his guns by means of a map reference, while the CPO and others in the division check and, if necessary, correct this information. All this action has to take place each time a gun position is changed. This means that if necessary, all seventy-two guns in the division could engage the same target. This ability was used, very successfully, on a number of occasions in northwest Europe.

All this means that the gunners are in so many ways kept in the dark as to what is happening. They never see their targets and have to be informed as to what success has been achieved. So the actual training was so important in building up complete confidence between these entities. There also needs to be a complete rapport between the Troop Commander and his infantry counterpart. Quite obviously, the sooner the gunner can bring fire to bear, exactly where the infantryman wants it and in the quantity required, the sooner does this mutual trust develop.

Within a few nights of landing we had our first casualty. One of our Troop Commanders was in a semi derelict tower as an observation post. A German gun scored a direct hit, and he was killed. We were undergoing shell and mortar fire on odd occasions, but nothing too severe. After one fairly hairy night, I had orders to take all my men, in small groups as they could be spared, to a certain position on our left. Not having the vaguest idea why this order had been given, I took the first group myself. The sight before us was certainly an upsetting one. In a very small, shallow slit-trench a figure was crouched, bending forward. He was the victim of enemy shell fire. The back of his neck had been sliced open and a large lump gouged out. To say that it was not a pretty sight is a complete understatement. The lesson to all of us was when under shell fire to dig deep and dig quick. It was the simplest and most salutary lesson I was ever to receive. I know that that poor fellow's death, in those circumstances, was to save many.

For weeks we moved around, forward, sideways, whatever the orders were. We were constantly in action and our men grew weary. However we knew that our foothold on the continent was continually being improved, strengthened and enlarged, but the infantry had to fight hard for whatever ground they gained.

Caen

One of our moves was to a spot overlooking Caen. The Canadians had been attacking it for quite a while, but the stubborn resistance still held them out. Our job was to reinforce the attack which had been relying on air power with our 25 pounders so we could bring some powerful and accurate firepower to bear and give the defenders a real headache. An enormous amount of shells were thrown into the city and the destruction was enormous. In some respects this was a double edged sword as the Germans actually used the ruined buildings to their advantage for constructing strong points in the ruins. With the additional firepower from a number of our units, the infantry eventually triumphed. The following day we drove through Caen to our new position. Groups of desultory and obviously shell shocked German defenders were still being formed up and taken into captivity. As regards the town itself I have never seen a more desolate scene. Caen had been subjected to the fire of numerous artillery units for days on end, as well as a number of bomber attacks. There were still some civilians living there and the entire place, buildings and humans, seemed to have a thick coating of dirty grey dust. It was really a heartbreaking sight.

The whole of July went by. We, as gunners, really had it easy compared to how the infantry were faring. We moved from A to B and then to C, but they were just open areas, with one spot being like any other. But we knew from the amount of firing we did to support the infantry that they were having a very busy and dangerous time. A little news kept filtering down about how they were faring, and about the losses. Sometimes light, sometimes heavy, but seldom none. But virtually every incident in which they took part resulted in victory, some taking longer than others. Eventually the effect really began to tell on the enemy.

Falaise

Two incidents from this period stick in my mind, one fairly humorous, and the other obviously not. To the rear of one of my gun positions near Falaise, quite some distance away, was a fairly dark looking object. I decided to investigate – carefully. To my surprise it was the front portion of an RAF bomber. There were three crew members still inside, in a mummified state. I chose not to move them, but notify the War Graves Commission of their exact location so that they could be properly cared for.

The other occasion concerned my Troop Sergeant Major. We were doing one of our night drives. We were all absolutely shattered; we'd had very little sleep. We were halted, just waiting events when TSM Dilley (who was a real old soldier of many years' service) came out of his jeep and begged me to take over the driving of his vehicle so that he might have a short nap in the back of my truck. He was sure that he'd fall asleep otherwise. I acquiesced, and changed vehicles. Another lad came and joined me as my passenger. After quite a while the signal to proceed was given. As soon as the jeep moved I knew I'd been stung. There was a puncture in one of the back wheels. In a jeep the tools are kept in small boxes on top of the back wheels. The back of the jeep was absolutely crammed with stuff which we had to move before we could reach the tool boxes. After that we had to change the wheel, and all the while the regiment was getting further away, and we had no idea where we were heading. These night drives were simply follow my leader and keep hoping. Of course old Dilley swore that he was perfectly innocent. "The puncture must have happened after I stopped." he said. He certainly never had the same chance to catch me again.

The race into Belgium

We sped, on until late in August we crossed the Seine near Rouen. Then early in September we crossed the Somme at Picquigny, a few miles from Amiens, then on to Saint Fol and Bethune. It was here that another incident occurred.

I was a member of a small 'recce' (Reconnaissance) party. I was dropped off by myself to go into an adjacent field and make preparations for the arrival of the guns which would follow on in a few hours. I did not have long for it to get a little lighter so that I could start my preparations. Away to my right I could see the faint outlines of a few houses, I then noticed a slight stationary figure watching me. He began approaching slowly and I could see that he was wearing light mauve breeches, resembling a farmer. He was very hesitant until it became a little lighter and he could see me more clearly. Then he ran towards me quite excitedly. He asked if I was 'Anglais' and when I replied yes he embraced me and sobbed. I was able to assure him that the Germans had retreated from the whole area and were miles away. He then left me and ran towards the little hamlet and shouted madly until everyone was awake and had heard the good news. People began rushing towards me, dressing as they came. It was then for the first time that it really sank in as to how these people had suffered through years of occupation. I was being smothered by them all and to cap it all, my guns began to arrive. I had to beg them to stand clear while the guns were put into their positions.

All that day I was being grabbed by people who simply had to shake my hand or kiss me. They spent the whole day talking to the lads and looking at the guns. It was fortuitous that we had no firing instructions otherwise I don't know what would have happened. Late in the afternoon a shy young girl, hanging onto her parents hands, shyly handed me a 'photo' of herself, on the back of which she had written, in French, 'Souvenir of the day of my Liberation, Bethune, 5th Sept. 1944. Emilienne Cousin'. Due to the good auspices of a newspaper editor in LIEGE, in Sept 1994, I again met Emilienne with her husband and little grand-daughter. They were accompanied by the daughter of the first man to see me that day, as well as her husband. Unfortunately the man himself was dead.

Walcheren

Anyway, back to the main story. We carried on through Armentieres and as far as Antwerp in Belgium. The armoured Div. had driven in and the 53rd Div. were the first foot-soldiers to enter. The area of Antwerp, South of the Albert canal was free of Germans, but they were settled on the North bank and on the Walcheren Islands in the estuary. We were given our gun positions, but things were pretty quiet. We now saw our first real signs of civilisation since landing in France. There were shops open, actually selling things!!

I was dumbfounded to see rich-looking cream cakes on sale. There was a beautiful public bathing pool with one large retractable wall that opened up to flood the pool with sunshine. It was a wonderful break to walk around the streets with so little damage evident. But soon the Germans began the odd spot of shelling onto the town itself. We had arrived in Antwerp on the 8th September and were to move out around the 15th September starting the operation to drive a narrow corridor up through Holland to the Nijmegen area.

We had now gone through two spheres of war. In Normandy we had experienced a very enclosed type of feeling, which had been completely changed after the 'breakout'. As people who manned the guns, we were never able to see our targets or even know what our targets actually were. When things had quietened down, the T.C. would be able to put us in the picture to some extent. We were usually told how the battle had progressed. Normally we would only be aware that we were in some field and that the enemy would be somewhere in front of us. Our memories of the various, numerous gun positions which we had occupied were therefore very vague and were defined only by the conditions which we had been forced to endure in. For example, in some we had been subjected to an objectionable amount of enemy shell-fire or rocket-fire. The horrible experiences were, at night, being subjected to action from the 'Moaning Minnies' which is what we called their multiple rocket-launchers. As the rockets flew towards you, they set up a hideous very loud screaming sound!! Not very pleasant! Fortunately, they didn't happen too often. After the 'breakout' we were at least able to see signs of humanity and even the odd civilian.

Operation Garden

Field Marshall Montgomery planned that his troops, the 21st Army Group would force a narrow corridor, the length of Holland and would arrive at Nijmegen on the river Waal. This operation started about the 17th September and my unit was part of XII Corps who were on the left flank of the Operation. Later in the year we were transferred to XXX Corps so I had the honour of serving with two famous formations. As the world knows, the operation was not completely successful. We eventually took Nijmegen and our Battery was positioned on the 'Island' between Nijmegen and Arnhem for quite some time. We were firing in support of the paratroops still fighting around Oosterbreek. The ground forces who formed the Operation Garden part of the action knew what we had to do and we gave it everything we could but as history records it wasn't quite enough. It's a testament to the herculean efforts of the supply companies that we were able to provide a great deal of artillery cover in support of the actions going on around Oosterbreek and

Cromwell tanks of Guard's Armoured Division drive along 'Hell's Highway' towards Nijmegen during Operation 'Market-Garden', 20 September 1944

also on the road which is now known as Hell's Highway. This whole operation had been accompanied by the fiercest artillery fire of the war. In 24 hours, each of my four guns had fired the unbelievable sum of one thousand rounds. This works out at approximately one shell per gun every one and half minutes without a break. The actual events of the battle are now something of a blur and on the ground in the thick of things it's impossible to gain a clear picture of what is going on around you, but my enduring memory is the need to constantly move and acquire new targets in what was obviously a very fluid and mobile action.

I must mention here that whilst waiting to cross the bridge to the 'Island', I dismounted from my vehicle to stretch my legs, and who happened to be on the pavement, but Eric Melton, an old school chum who was now a member of the R.A.M.C in the Polar Bear division. A quick chat and we were on our respective ways. Such was life!

On the 17 October we withdrew from the 'Island' and went S.W. of Grave whilst liberation of Hertogenbosch was planned. This city was the capital of the large area of North Brabant which now had to be taken to protect the narrow corridor which had been created. It was known that the city was extremely well defended because it protected vital German supply routes.

At 6:30am on the 22nd October this memorable battle started. Five tremendous days of battle followed and eventually on the evening of the 27th, all resistance was virtually defunct. Hard-fought battles took place at dozens of vital points and each individual battle was costly. During October the division lost; 145 men killed, 705 men wounded and 83 men missing. These were principally suffered at Den Bosch. On the 24th October a platoon of the 1/5th Welch fought their way over a Canal Bridge. They were initially menaced by a S.P. gun, (self propelled). Soon two more S.P.'s supported the first. In the meantime the bridge behind them had been destroyed. Many were killed and by evening the survivors were taken prisoner.

The gallant gentleman in charge of this platoon was Capt. (later Major) David Ronald Morgan. Since the arrival in Normandy in June, it has been estimated that the infantry have been out of contact with the enemy for only four days. The Press, back home, recorded this victory as a tremendous success for the Division! Ever since, the people of Den Bosch and those of the 53rd. have built up and maintained the greatest rapport. They have a 53rd. War Memorial there, and there is a simple 53rd Div. Cross in the Cathedral of St. Jan.

Most of November and the first half of December was spent in the area of Roermond and Venlo on the river Maas. It was possibly classed as a fairly quiet period, but there were numerous skirmishes both sides of the river.

We were now to be withdrawn in order to rest, refit and carry out special training for future operations. We scarcely had time to draw breath at Bree, when an 'O' group was called (TO issue urgent orders). On the 16th December, the Germans had put in an attack in the Ardennes and thus initiated the 'Battle of the Bulge'. The next day we had a pitiful premature Christmas dinner. The ration of turkey was said to be two ounces per man! Whether this was live or dead weight, I don't know, it's the only figure I heard quoted. The ration was so painful; the officers said they would forego this wonderful share-out. I mention later, the fact that I witnessed an American Christmas dinner. So, we set out for the Ardennes to help our wonderful American Allies. The weather had turned really cold and when we got there our gun position was completely snow-covered. The only extra equipment which we'd received to help us fight the wintry conditions was a petty little one-person sleeping tent issued to each of us. The temperature was basically below freezing and the wind was biting. Due to the atrocious conditions, there were many road accidents, so the Americans had introduced 'Wrecker Gangs', which patrolled the area in their lorries and dealt with all damaged and abandoned vehicles.

One day the Major from a sister Battery called in to telephone his unit. On the road in front of my troop, just around a corner his Jeep had a puncture and had no spare wheel available. So he had contacted his unit to send a vehicle with men and a spare wheel to see to his Jeep. It seemed absolute ages before the relief vehicle arrived and reported that they could not find the Jeep. I won't say what the Major called the 'idiots', who had passed his vehicle and were too blind to see it. All they ever found was a body of a Jeep. In about twenty minutes the 'Wreckers' had taken everything. The wheels, seats, engine and every working part had disappeared!

A picture taken in 1945 by Captain Davies of German prisoners being led into captivity past interested members of his gun troop.

It was actually then that we had to take over an American gun position. I went along first to gather all the technical information and my guns would follow later. Their 'cookhouse' was fifty yards or so behind the actual guns. I was talking to their Captain when one of his sergeants approached, carrying the large tray on which was his Christmas dinner. The Captain looked at it and said 'hardly worth walking back for'. As well as a mountain of goodies, that tray held a complete leg and several slices of turkey breast. That one G.I. had been given more turkey than my entire troop had received. I did wonder if we were fighting the same war.

My guns arrived and the Yanks were departing. I pointed out to the Captain that they had not yet picked up a mound of 60 to 80 pairs of brand new boots and a pile of almost 100 'Compo' packs. 'If they aren't in your way, we'll leave them'. How I managed to hide my enthusiasm, I just don't know. A 'compo' pack was a good-sized cardboard box which contained rations for seven men for three days. And what rations! Tins of bacon, corned beef hash, rich Christmas-style fruit puddings, the like of which we hadn't seen for years. Everything was fairly split between the four gun crews and the Command Post personnel. We all managed to find a pair of boots to fit, and were able to have a second breakfast for ages. The extra food certainly helped us to cope with the shocking conditions. Snow, cold, wet and we were living in the open air. No accommodation of any kind. One evening David Thomson, my troop Commander came down from his O.P. (Observation Post). He was absolutely over the moon. He had just received a telegram to let him know that his wife had given birth to a daughter – their first child, and both were well.

Whilst in Antwerp I had managed to purchase a few miniatures of Benedictine. On exceptionally cold nights, when firing was necessary, I had shared the odd tot with my Command Post Crew, just a little sip each to keep the cold at bay. That night we used them all to ensure that Mother and child were properly 'toasted'. Diana's birthday was the 28th December.

Very early one morning I saw something which I shall never forget. In each of our vehicles, on the passenger side there is a circular hole in the roof (a Bren gun ring) so the passenger can stand up and observe. We were travelling North with a very deep river valley on our left and beyond that a mountain which was a little higher than the one on which we were travelling. Dawn was not very far away. Although we remained in darkness, a beam of light shone across the valley and illuminated a scene of the Crucifixion on the opposite side. The three figures on the crosses were beautifully colourful and the whole scene sparkled and glittered. I wondered how many coincidences had to coincide for us to be exactly there at that exact moment. The whole world was in darkness except for that scene. It was worth going to the Ardennes if only to see that.

The great worry of the Ardennes was now over, so we were all travelling back to the small village of Embourg which was very near Liege. However, David and I had to stay behind in

Namur to give evidence in a Court-Martial. We had to report to the American Town-Major to be allocated accommodation. We were taken to the Chateau of a Titled Belgian Diplomat. He was stuck in occupied France, his wife and children were in Namur. The butler came to our room to tell us that the Countess was inviting us to join her for dinner. We knew that food was in very short supply, so we gave him two tins of corned beef from our rations. The chef concocted a lovely meal from the bully beef and the countess asked the butler what on earth the main course was. When he explained, the poor lady burst into tears, they hadn't seen meat for ages. Two days later, David and I set off in an open Jeep to Embourg. It was absolutely freezing and on the way we saw a queue of G.I.s at a truck on the roadside. It was a P.X. (like our NAAFI). We asked if we could join and the answer was a generous affirmative and we grabbed our mugs from the Jeep. We then saw that the G.I. s all had sticks and mugs. We then watched as each G.I. took his turn , held his stick so that the P.X. lady put ring doughnuts on stick, as many as it would hold. They quickly found us a stick each and there was strictly no charge. This truck would visit them weekly, conditions permitting.

We had been overseas more than six months and in the whole of that time we had seen one NAAFI van from which we had been allowed to purchase one cup of tea and one temporary pack of biscuits.

Embourg was a delightful little village. Our Mess was in a fairly large house on top of a hill. My billet, mainly for sleeping, was in a lovely detached house owned by M. Auguste Liesken. He was a metallurgist in the Steel Works in Liege and having travelled extensively in U.S.A., spoke excellent English. He had two young children and each evening they moved to his parent's house where they slept. This was because this other house had a substantial cellar and although no 'flying bombs' had actually landed in the village, they did occasionally fly overhead. We had about ten days rest in Embourg which was absolute heaven after six months of almost continuous action and sleeping in the open. To stroll into the local Café and order a coffee and aperitif was like being in a new world. Struggling to talk to the locals was an extra bonus.

However, all good things come to an end and so we moved back up North to the Helmond area – at least for a few days. We had left the Ardennes on the 10th Jan and we were about to leave Embourg on the 17th. Two incidents stick in my mind from Embourg. Firstly, Auguste Liesken was able to pass me enough knowledge on his theory that the flying bombs launching pads were limited in number, and had such a small traverse that Embourg did not come within their sphere of operation. We went around the village publicising this fact to such good effect that the elders agreed that it would be safe to hold a dance one night. No one had been out in the dark lately because of the bomb menace. Needless to say, the dance was a tremendous success.

The other event was not a pleasant one. Stuart Shrimpton had been a Captain since the war started. He now had the misfortune to break his ankle in an accident. The rules were such that after 21 days in hospital, he had to revert to the rank of Lieutenant! We were all disgusted at this but there was nothing we could do. This was the way the Army treated it's wounded. Almost unbelievable!!

After a few fairly quiet days at Helmond, we found that our next target was the Reichwald Forest, a part of the very strong Siegfried Line. At Helmond we had civilian billets. With one other, I was billeted with a Frau Stockerman and her teenage daughter Loni, this of course being a Dutch family. We explained as well as we could that all we needed was a bedroom which we could share and we would be having all our meals elsewhere. We just couldn't fathom the terrified state in which both the females were.

Fortunately, some of our lads in the next billet were able to tell us that Frau Stockerman was not a widow as we had assumed, but that her husband was actually a German by birth. When the Germans had found out when they invaded, they had taken him for the army, completely against his wishes. I made haste to find a local who could assure the poor females that they were in no danger at all from us and we genuinely sympathised with their position. The atmosphere finally cleared.

The Army now intended attacking the area S.E. of Nijmegen between the rivers Rhine and Maas. This was where the Siegfreid Line was, and the 53rd Div. was given the unenviable task of clearing out the Reichwald Forest. On the 8th Feb the battle started with a tremendous Artillery barrage. More than one thousand guns were said to be engaged in it. The hard frost conditions had broken and conditions underfoot were now very wet and heavy. The troops fought their way in atrocious conditions, but by the next evening, the 9th, all the first objectives had been taken. Ground conditions were so bad that all kinds of vehicles, including tanks, were getting completely bogged down and unable to move. The infantry kept advancing regardless, sometimes against very heavy opposition and also determined counter-attacks.

At times like these the Artillery support was particularly vital. The flooding had created such atrocious conditions that at one time, or so we were told, that of the 72 field guns in the Division, only 12 were capable of giving support fire. Of these, 8 were the guns of 497 Bty!!

At this time poor Dick Potter (who was G.P.O. of ETroop), had a foot blown off by a Schu mine. What made it worse was that an ambulance couldn't get through, so we had to wait for a Weasel (a small tracked vehicle). It was said afterwards that under the prevailing weather conditions the successful attack by the men of the 53rd Welsh Division was an operation unique in military history. By the 17th – 18th Feb, enemy resistance, fortunately, was waning and the troops were having a slightly easier time. On the 20th Feb GOCH was captured. (This was the first anniversary of my father's death). But the men had to push further south and again the intensity increased.

On one day I had a memorable diversion. My troop was on the right of the road, opposite; on the left was a Medium Bty. As the day progressed we were aware of dozens of Highland Infantry being placed at something like 10 yard intervals along the length of the road. We soon found out that Winston Churchill was expected and he wanted to fire a shell across the Rhine into the heart of Germany. His car arrived, he stepped out, dressed as a full Colonel and wearing his 'British Warm'. I raced across the road to see it all. The gun was already loaded and aimed. All the great man needed to do was to step forward and pull the lanyard. A young subaltern stepped forward and offered him a set of ear-plugs. With a grand Churchillian gesture the articles were brushed aside. The lanyard was pulled, the gun fired and a great roar of approval rose. As he left, he was within two feet of me and I could clearly see that both ears were absolutely stuffed with cotton wool! The man was quietly smiling to himself. I thought 'What a performance'.

By the 11th March the Div. had completed its tasks and was waiting to withdraw. Between the 8th February and the 7th March the Div. had suffered 1229 battle casualties and 3200 prisoners captured. More than 180 000 rounds of 25pdr. had been fired. The next big task would be to attempt the Rhine crossing.

Perhaps I could explain here that very often when a small number of Infantry were about to engage the enemy, a very large quantity if Artillery could be called upon to give support. This was very often of real significance in reducing casualties. Each Infantry Division contained three Artillery Regts. of Field Gunners, i.e. 25pdrs. This gave a total of 72 guns available. However, sometimes, when a single Battalion of Infantry was involved in an attack, it may be deemed necessary to give them the enhanced support of, maybe four Divisions' Artillery. For example, the combined firing power of 288 guns. Even this lot may have the power of heavier Artillery added to them.

Around the 12th March, it was envisaged that this enhanced power would be needed. So on that date all the Divisional Infantry began a move to the Brussels area to have a period of rest, refitting and preparation for the next operation. We gunners stayed put and kept on firing.

I must take time now to recount this tale: Some time previously, when we were about to advance through what had once been a hunting country we received orders that on no account were we to attempt to shoot game. It seemed so incongruous that the authorities would see fit to take time to issue such an order in the middle of a War, but issue it they did. On this particular day the guns were situated just in front of a wood. To our left-rear were more trees and one stretch of 'fire-break'. The peace was broken by the sound of a rifle-shot. I rushed out to investigate. One of my gun-sergeants, Bryn Button was waving his rifle in the air and shouting that he had made a mistake and there was no danger. I approached him and he claimed that he had just finished cleaning his rifle and was clearing the chamber when it went off and he had accidentally and very unfortunately killed this poor little deer that happened to be crossing the small open stretch at that time. It wouldn't have done to leave the carcass to rot, so I agreed that Bryn could cut the carcass up and divide it into five shares, one for each of the guns and one share for the Command Post. Now I was the proud possessor of two little paraffin stoves, which were used for odd little feeding jobs. We had acquired a large 'Ali-Baba' jar, which was now almost filled with isinglass in which we preserved our egg stocks. Bryn now quietly approached me and said that he had been able to hold back a few nice venison steaks. The arrangements were quickly made. When he and I were both on night duty, I should start cooking and once things were virtually ready, I would simply pick up the Tannoy and say 'Sergeant Button, to the Command Post immediately please' and Bryn would double across with his plate stuffed inside his blouse!!!

The crossing was to begin on the night 23/24 March. We were now very near the Rhine, near Rees and Xanten. We were putting in preparatory fire on targets which had been selected. We saw airborne troops dropping on the far side of the Rhine. One plane had dropped its troops and was hit after turning around for home. The crew baled out. One was blown across the Rhine and was landing right alongside my Command Post. This fellow landed with his eyes shut tight and shouting 'Kamerad'. He didn't realise that he had blown across to 'our' side, but was convinced that he was about to become a P.O.W.

His relief was unbounded and he insisted that we have some of his surplus items of clothing as gifts. He didn't look a day over 18. It was probably on the 26th March 1945 that we crossed the Rhine on the Bailey Bridge at Xanten. The Infantry kept advancing and enlarging the bridgehead. It was very hot work at the guns which were firing day and night. After a tremendous battle, the town of Bocholt which had been strongly defended was eventually captured by the evening of the 29th. There were further river crossings ahead and the enemy was managing to blow the bridges as they retired, thus causing our Infantry further delays. By the 31st Mar the town of Vreden was occupied, about 30 miles from the Rhine. On the 2nd April, Gronau was taken.

Things didn't really get easier but things, in some way became looser. For a while, after reaching the Dortmund - Ems Canal in the first week of April, the Division hardly ever acted as a whole and individual Brigades, or even smaller units undertook separate tasks. Continually pressing forward we crossed the Aller and Weser rivers near Verden.

By the 4th April the Brigade had captured the Airfield just West of Rhine and by the following morning of the following day the Division was established on a line from Gronau –

Ochtrup - Salzbergen line, holding the Northern flank as far as the Dortmund-Ems Canal, having advanced about 75 miles since crossing the Rhine. There was considerable resistance by the enemy in the area around Ibbenburen and the Div. Artillery was used extensively. Elsewhere resistance was patchy, casualties correspondingly lighter and advances quicker.

On the 7th April we were to join 7th Armoured at Hoya. When our troops attempted to cross the Aller at Rethem, they met tremendous resistance, so the attempt was postponed and attempts would be made elsewhere. However, within a few days the enemy had, to a large extent; withdrawn so the Aller was crossed at Rethem and Western on the 13th April.

It was considered that Bremen would be a tough nut to attack directly, so the 53rd was to push North and capture Verden, then to continue North so as to cut off Bremen from any communication with the East. Verden was captured on the 17th April. We spent the next week or so operating in the Soltau area. On the 24th we were to advance to try an attack and cut the Bremen-Hamburg autobahn at a point near Elsdorf. For a while we met stiff opposition, and then we were to turn West and advance on Bremen. However, resistance in Bremen collapsed, so we halted. On the night of 29/30th April, the Brigade relieved 11th Armoured on the Elbe near Winsen. On the 2nd May, we began passing through a bridgehead created across the Elbe by the 15th Scottish Div. The Division began to enter at dawn on the 4th May. Our particular billet area was in Harburg which was a suburb of Hamburg, situated on the South of the Elbe.

On the 4th May 1945, all enemy forces in North Germany were surrendered to Field – Marshall Sir Bernard Montgomery on Luneburg Heath!!!!

It has been written 'The Welsh Division enjoyed a series of uninterrupted successes. They never lost a battle or failed in any major task entrusted to them'.

CHAPTER 3:

THE GERMAN VIEW OF OPERATION MARKET

The German view of the battle for Arnhem was coloured by the heavy hand of censorship and the political agenda of Goebels' propaganda ministry. The defeat of the British paratroops forming the outermost spearhead of Operation Market offered a rare opportunity for the media of hard pressed Third Reich to boast of a German victory.

Embedded with the German Wehrmacht and Waffen SS forces were the Kereigsberichter (or war reporters) these men attached the various units known as Propaganda Komponien (Propaganda Companies). The man on the spot in Arnhem was a Wehrmacht Kreigberichter by the name of Erwin Kirchhof (1919-1979). This is the official English translation of the newspaper account filed by Herr Kirchhof which was widely reprinted throughout Germany. It is written in the typical bombastic Third Reich style and has been heavily sub-edited but serves a fascinating primary source of how the German population were served up news on the home front in 1944.

The Fight of the Elite: The story of how the First British Airborne Division was destroyed

This is the story of how the First British Airborne Division was destroyed. (From a PK-special report for "The Westkurier" by the War Reporter Erwin Kirchhof.)

"Finally the assignment that we have been waiting for has been given to us. It is an airborne landing on the greatest scale with the purpose of clearing the way for the Second British Army through Holland to Northern Germany. Each and every soldier must know the importance of these bridges. These under all circumstances must be kept intact for the army that is to follow. This may possible be our last job. Let us all make the best of this opportunity."

Extracted from the Order of the Day of the British Divisional Commander.

On the morning of September 17th only minor activities were reported along the Albert and Maas Schelde Canal. But this resulted in the greatest activity of Field Marshal Model's headquarters. During the last 14 days of uninterrupted offensives the British 2nd Army had tried with the concentrated striking power of more than 12 divisions to break through the German positions stretched behind the barricades of the streams and canals of Southern Holland, in order to push through Holland and to reach Northern Germany.

The very heavy air attacks on airports and traffic installations in the plain of the Lower Rhine and other indications pointed to Eisenhower's intention to break the stalemate and continue his

The surviving German self propelled artillery elements of II SS Panzer Corps were on hand to add weight to the battle for the shrinking perimeter at the north end of Arnhem bridge.

push. For that he would use all the forces he had assembled in England since the beginning of the invasion.

Where would the enemy try to surprise us?

It was an early Sunday afternoon. The cinemas in the small Dutch towns were slowly filling up, and the streets and highways along the canals and small streams, were crowded with young people on bicycles. And then out of the blue sky roared several hundred enemy fighter bombers. Their aim was to attack the German defensive positions and locate the flak positions. Barely had they disappeared beyond the horizon when, coming from the west across the flooded coastal areas, appeared the planes and gliders carrying regiments and brigades of the enemy's airborne army. They were flying low. They were headed by the four-motored transport planes, loaded with parachute battalions. Following them, came the two-motored tow-planes of the large cargo gliders. Our flak batteries, which had refrained from firing at the fighter bombers, now opened up with all they had at the close flying formations. Each and every soldier of the line and even the headquarters personnel and the cooks helped. Split up into two fleets, the enemy's formations turned before Eindhoven and Arnhem in a large circle towards each other. The first parachute landings were made on a front of about 70 kilometres and approximately 100 kilometres behind our lines. The troops bailed out from a very low altitude, sometimes as low as 60 metres. Immediately after that the several hundred gliders started to land. In these first few minutes it looked as if the downcoming masses would suffocate every single life on the ground. Coinciding with these mass landings behind our lines the enemy started to attack with increased ferocity on the whole line along the Albert and Maas Schelde Canal and on both sides of Aachen. His armoured columns, the backbone of his strategy, were ordered to start the push again.

Shortly after the landings of the British and American

divisions, our recce troops went into action. By searching the countless forests and large parks in that area, cut by numerous small streams, they had to ascertain where the enemy intended to concentrate his forces: only then could a basis for our counter attacks be established. The telephone lines were cut. The recce cars could move forward only slowly. Some of the enemy dug themselves in near their landing places and brought weapons into position. Others moved up to the houses and barricaded themselves, using the furniture inside the buildings. From there they tried to dominate our bridges and beat back our counter attacks. Elements of the Dutch population assisted the enemy in their task. An SS-Obersturmfuhrer and bearer of the "Ritterkreuz" was on reconnaissance near Arnhem, when he collided in a forest road with one of the enemy's jeeps. Before the British Lieutenant and his 3-man team recovered from the surprise, they were captured. From their personal papers, it was clear that they belonged to the 1st British Airborne Division and had taken part in the campaigns in Africa, Sicily and Italy. They wore red berets and called themselves "Red Devils". Now they blamed themselves for not being more careful and doing their job better. SS Obersturmfuhrer "G", after a drive of several hours in his reconnaissance car, reached the Arnhem bridge and crossed it to the southern bank. His reconnaissance had constantly been interrupted by air attacks. The German guards on both sides of the bridge had hardly suffered any casualties. There was no trace of the several hundred men who had landed nearby. All of a sudden a steady stream of machine gun bullets hit the centre of the bridge, coming from the direction of the southern bank. The bearer of the "Ritterkreutz" was hit. An SS Unterscharfuhrer took over. In the late hours of the same evening he was able to report to the SS Obersturmbannfuhrer, now the Kamfgruppe Commander: "The strength of the enemy that landed is approximately 3,000 men supported by heavy weapons which include 7.65cm AT guns and 15cm infantry howitzers and light armoured vehicles. They landed in the area west of Arnhem between the rail road tracks and the Rhine River, reaching the line Wolfheze, south of the Rhine and on both sides of the highway from Arnhem-Ede, 6km northwest of Arnhem. The enemy intends to hold the Rhine bridge until he can establish contact with Montgomery's army."

The areas in which the landing of the First Airborne Division occurred had a width of 10km and a depth of 12km. SS Obersturnbannfuhrer H, a giant-like officer who has never lost his wits, even in the most hopeless situation of a battle, acted as general staff officer and dynamic commander. Together with the commander of an SS Pz Corps who also is an energetic personality, he forged the steel pocket of Arnhem. In the cold and rainy night the town was entirely cut off, particularly from the northwest. On the morning of the 18th September the SS units arrived from the north to reinforce the Northwestern part of the pocket. In line, northwest of Arnhem, near Ede, the Alarmeinheiten (Alarm Units) attacked. These units consisted of soldiers from every part of the earth. The attack was towards the East. The British at this time were receiving two Parachute Battalions and numerous airborne units, including more heavy weapons, as reinforcements, but they realised that encirclement threatened them. They dug in even deeper, they used every bush and every tree for cover, they converted every building into a strongpoint bristling with weapons. They were all volunteers and members of British regiments with a long and victorious tradition. The majority of them were officers and NCO's. The German troops who beat those first-rate British troops back, metre for metre, inflicting heavy casualties on them in close hand to hand fighting, were men of every branch of the service. Only 24 hours before they had not known each other: the aeroplane technicians still worked on their planes: the soldiers of the Waffen SS were refitting their units in a small Dutch village; the

Landesschutzen units were still employed as guards on military objectives; the naval coast artillery men had just returned from their strong points; the boys from the R&D were still constructing field positions. Only a few of them were familiar with the principles of fighting in forest and hedge-row or street fighting. But they fought. In one infantry battalion members of as many as 28 different units fought side by side. Their Battalion Commander was a Ritterkreuzertrager and also the bearer of the golden Verwundetenabzeichen. He was a Captain with a wooden leg. Yet this particular battalion fought as one of the best and the most fanatical. The thoughts of their fatherland drove them forward, lending them miraculous strength.

On the German left flank the attacks came to a halt about midday. The enemy had set up a well camouflaged Anti-tank position in the forest, flanked and surrounded by numerous MG's and snipers. Even the assault guns could not break through. Several times they tried to roll up from behind the positions of the 7.65cm long-barrelled AT guns, but the British recognised the danger every time and established the anti-tank guns on the threatened flanks, using their fast-moving vehicles. All the German attacks were unsuccessful. Then an SS Unterscharfuhrer together with a handful of men, armed only with a few hand grenades, worked themselves up to the front of their positions, up to the AT gun positions. They overpowered the crews and the German attack rolled on.

On the right flank, between the railroad tracks and the Rhine, in the residential suburbs of Oosterbeek, the struggle for each building continued for hours. In the narrow streets, hand grenades were thrown from one side of the street to the other. Further down the Northern bank of the Rhine the fight for the buildings from which the enemy dominated the bridge with his guns had continued since dawn. Hand to hand fighting raged on each floor of the houses. In the power station on the Oost Straat men of the Luftwaffe mounted to the first floor and exchanged hand grenades with the British on the floor above.

In the evening a British radio message was intercepted in which a battalion commander, barricaded with four hundred of his paratroopers in the buildings along the Rhine bridge, asked for the dropping of masonry tools and cement. He intended to build a defensive wall around his positions.

The battles raged deep into the raining night.

The encirclement must be broken

19th September. SS Obersturmbannfuhrer H, day and night at the front with his men, now himself led the sharp thrust to the left of the right wing, covering the north western edge of Arnhem. The same day he made contact with the left flank, arriving from the west. The British Airborne Division was now encircled in an area of only a few square kilometres, between the railroad line and the Rhine. While under heavy enemy fire, the light flak guns broke up an enemy thrust. Only a few minutes later, the same guns shot down seven fighter bombers. The enemy received reinforcements of two para battalions, one of them Polish and several glider units. German fighters and flak inflicted heavy losses on the escaping enemy planes. Even Radio London admits that the German Luftwaffe in the whole Dutch area was as active on that day as in their days of glory. Artillery and mortar batteries hammered the pocket. Around noon, two British envoys asked for a one hour armistice to take more than six hundred casualties into German hospitals. Their proposal was accepted. A doctor of the Waffen SS and a British doctor supervised the transport. Afterwards there were further heavy attacks by the enemy. The number of prisoners rose to 904. Among them was the Divisional Commander. Several armoured automatic weapons, 50 trucks and light tanks and numerous weapons were captured.

20th September. The period of bad weather kept up. Between

the railroad track and the Rhine heavy house to house fighting continued in and around Oosterbreek.

Our flak shot down 10 supply planes. The major part of the weapons and food containers fell into our hands. This was caused by concentrated defensive fire. Fierce dog fights took place over the battle area. Our own fighters attacked the enemy on the ground. The enemy bombing attacks did not hit our mortar batteries. The enemy fired on Oosterbeek, directed by the infantry. It generally took four minutes from the call for fire support until the first shells landed. Again the enemy handed over more than 800 wounded in a period of armistice. The number of prisoners was now well over 2000.

21st September. The British Division again received several hundred reinforcements and attempted in desperation to break the ring of iron; but despite this, we compressed the pocket still further. The size of the pocket was now an area of 1200 metres by 750 metres. Mortars, artillery and flak fired into the forests and into the positions in the streets. Again 700 wounded were handed over to us. The number of dead was by now extremely high. Our light and medium flak was forced to destroy every single building on the southern bank of the Rhine. Opposite the power station, where a strong force of enemy paratroops were holding out, the officer directing the fire of a medium flak battery established his position. Even though he realised that the first shells might hit him, he called for fire on the power station. The first salvo seriously wounded him. The next brought down the large building. After the enemy charged three times at point blank range from Obst Street, he was mowed down. An SS Unterscharfuhrer escaped from the enemy and reported that 180 Germans were being held prisoner in the Tennis Court at Arnhem; ten metres in front of an AT and mortar position of Bn HQ!! For days they had not received any food. They fed themselves with beets, potatoes and ersatz coffee. Many were deprived of their valuables. The Unterscharfuhrer had useful information for the mortars. The enemy again suffered many casualties.

The Last Hours. In the following days Eisenhower continued to send new parachute battalions and glider units to the encircled remnants of the British Division. On the south side of the lower Rhine, between Nijmegen and Arnhem, a Polish Parachute Brigade landed with the task of breaking open the ring. Their attacks failed. Then the American General Dempsey was again ordered to break through to Arnhem from the south with his armoured columns and to contact the British. Only a few of his tanks managed to break into the German encirclement. They were soon destroyed by our medium flak guns. The enemy's air force was over the battle area at all times with light and heavy bomber squadrons, but strong German fighter formations and massed flak batteries prevented the enemy from attaining any real success. From inside the ring the hard-hit enemy attacked desperately day and night. By the 23rd September they had already sustained several thousand casualties. In addition, about 2000 wounded had already been transferred to German hospitals.

In London they spoke of the crisis of the Lower Rhine, but it was hoped that Dempsey would succeed in saving the remnants of the Division. During the night of 25/26 September, the First British Airborne Division, now only about 400 men strong, attempted to break through from Oosterbeek under cover of American covering fire and cross the Rhine. The British wrapped rags around their feet and crept over the asphalt roads to the Rhine bank. Suddenly German mortars caught them. Three, perhaps four, assault boats succeeded in reaching the opposite bank.

The OKW report of 27th September claimed that this elite British Division lost 6,450 PW's, thousands dead, 30 AT guns, additional guns and weapons and 250 trucks. In addition, 1000 gliders were destroyed or captured and more than 100 planes shot down.

CHAPTER 4

THE US 82ND AIRBORNE

"All American" is a small book covering the history of the 82nd Airborne Division. This book was one of the series of G.I. Stories published by the Stars & Stripes in Paris in 1944-1945. It contains a rather jingoistic account of the fighting but provides an accurate picture of how these events were presented to the US forces at the time.

The story of the 82nd Airborne Division

Airborne Division paratroopers tumbled from droning transports above the Nijmegen area. Troopers, and glidermen who followed, were veterans of Sicily, Italy, Normandy. This was the fourth combat jump for some; the second glider flight for others -- a record that still stands.

Landing more than 50 miles behind enemy lines, All-Americans were to blast a corridor through which the British Second Army could split Holland from the Albert Canal to Zuider Zee. The plan was designed to trap thousands of Germans troops to the west and blaze a path to the Fatherland.

The mission was in quadruplicate: to capture the Grave Bridge over the Maas River; to gain control of the huge "Gateway to Holland," Nijmegen Bridge, eight air miles northeast; to seize at least one span over the Maas-Waal Canal between Nijmegen and Grave; to take the highest ground in all Holland, at Berg En Dahl.

Official reports termed ground opposition to the 82nd's landing as "negligible." Such was hardly true as Pvt. Edwin C. Raub, Camp Lee, Va., 505th Parachute Inf., descended. With bullets ripping through his canopy, Raub slipped his 'chute to land near an AA gun. Without removing his harness, he killed one German, captured the crew, and disabled the gun.

Surprised Germans fled but were quick to rally. Fierce battles raged before "Mission Accomplished" was written into the records. Such was the Battle of Nijmegen which Columbia Broadcasting System Correspondent Bill Downs described as "...a single, isolated battle that ranks in magnificence and courage with Guam, Tarawa, Omaha Beach... a story that should be told to the blowing of bugles and the beating of drums for the men whose bravery made the capture of this crossing over the Waal River possible."

While the 504th Parachute Inf. made a daring, daylight crossing of the swift Waal in the face of direct machine gun and 40mm fire to take the north end of the bridge, a 505th battalion, aided by British tanks, swept through German defenses to capture the southern approach. Simultaneously, the 508th Parachute Inf. shouldered a Nazi counter-attack to the west, while the remainder of the 505th crushed another counter-thrust at Mook, seven miles south.

The 504th, under Col. Reuben H. Tucker, Ansonia, Conn., captured the Grave bridge in a dramatic fight. Troopers took over a flak tower, then turned its guns on a similar tower across the river. Men crossed in half sunken boats to remove demolitions from the bridge. The 508th grabbed Berg En Dahl and reached Nijmegen by nightfall. The 505th took Groesbeek and protected the south flank of the extended 82nd boundary.

All three regiments combined efforts to capture crossings over the Maas-Waal Canal Sept. 18. Except for the Nijmegen bridges, the 82nd's mission virtually was accomplished when contact was made with the British Guards Armd. Div. the next day. The Dutch Underground rendered invaluable assistance.

Division artillery glider elements and Special Troops glided in the second day. Some landing zones still were under enemy fire. It was men like 1st Sgt. Leonard A. Funk, Wilkinsburg, Pa., who kept glider landings from resembling another Normandy when counter-attacking Germans overran the 508th's drop zone, which also was the glider field.

Moving to the front of his company, the sergeant helped rally his men in a drive across 800 yards of open ground. Spotting four 20mm guns, Funk, with two others, attacked and destroyed each gun and crew. With glider landings imminent, he led a group to put three more AA guns out or action, killing more than 15 Germans.

Nijmegen Bridge was taken intact Sept. 20. Describing the assault, Downs reported:

"American Airborne infantry and British tanks beleaguered the streets of Nijmegen only 300 yards from the bridge that night, but they couldn't get it... A daring plan was drawn up. On Wednesday morning, the infantry (504th) made its way to the industrial outskirts along the river bank... British tanks protected troopers in street fighting, acted as artillery when the crossings were made...

"Twenty-six assault boats were in the water. Two hundred and sixty men would make the first assault. Waiting for them on the other bank were 400 to 600 Germans... the shelling continued. A smoke screen was laid, but it wasn't very effective because of the wind... Men slumped in their seats... of those 260 men, half were wounded or killed... only 13 of 26 boats came back... Others didn't wait for boats. Some stripped off equipment, took a bandolier of ammunition and swam the river, rifles on their backs.

"There was bitter bayonet fighting and Americans died, but more Germans died. That's only part of the story... British tanks and American Airborne Infantry (2nd Bn., 505th) began their frontal assault on the southern end of the bridge at the same time as the river crossing was started... Americans went through the houses on either side of the street.

"The southern end of the bridge has a large circular island

approach. In this island were four self-propelled guns. There was nothing to do but rush the guns. So the tanks lined up four abreast and all roared into the street, firing... the American Airborne troops and British tankmen seized the south end of the bridge. Only tanks could get across at first because half a dozen fanatical Germans remained high in the girders, sniping... The Nijmegen Bridge was in our hands intact as a monument to the gallantry of the 82nd Airborne soldiers, those who crossed the river, those who stormed it from the south."

Bitter fighting continued. The German Sixth Parachute Div. launched a coordinated attack toward Mook from the south and Berg En Dahl from the west. A full regiment drove a wedge into the two-mile front held by the remainder of the 505th. Positions were restored, however, within 24 hours.

Nazis also smacked the 508th after it had plunged into the flat lowlands of Germany at Wyler and Beek. The fierce assault swept within a short distance of Berg En Dahl, but a counter-attack threw the enemy from the hills and Beek was regained.

Pvt. John R. Towle, Tyrone, Pa., posthumously won the Congressional Medal of Honor when the enemy attacked the 504th's toehold north of the Waal with infantry and tanks Sept. 21. A bazookaman, Towle left his foxhole, crossed open ground under heavy fire and beat off tanks with rocket fire. He killed nine Germans with one round and was attacking a half-track when killed by a mortar shell. His action helped smother the German attack which not only threatened the bridgehead, but also thwarted relief of British paratroopers at Arnhem.

Delayed a week by bad weather, the 325th Glider Inf. landed Sept. 23 and immediately widened the corridor by ousting Germans from the Kiekberg woods. The enemy made only one more effort before settling back, attacking 508th positions in force Oct. 1. Artillery fire sprayed the division area, but the front was restored the next day.

Constant patrolling became the routine until Nov. 13 when

the division was relieved by Canadian troops. During this period, Pvt Bennie F. Siemanowicz, Nashau, N.H., 505th, observed two Germans for 10 days as they built a foxhole, roofed it with sheet metal and turf and prepared to settle down for the winter. One afternoon, Siemanowicz took off from his OP, crossed a mined bridge and ran along a dike to reach the prize foxhole. He exchanged shots with the startled Nazis, wounding one. Making the other carry his wounded companion, Siemanowicz returned under fire to his lines.

Division Commander James M. Gavin was promoted to major general in October. "Slim Jim," as his men called him, now got another nickname -- "The Two-Star Platoon Leader." First out of his plane on four combat jumps, the General specialized in close contact with his men. One of his aides, Capt. Hugo Olson, Cambridge, Minn., was wounded on two occasions while accompanying Gen. Gavin.

Following the 82nd's action in Holland, Lt. Gen. Sir Miles C. Dempsey, British Second Army Commander, paid this tribute to Gen. Gavin:

"I'm proud to meet the Commanding General of the greatest division in the world today."

CHAPTER 5

THE US 101ST AIRBORNE

Holland: Second D-Day for Screaming Eagles

Where next? This was the question in the mind of every Eagle trooper. By August, 1944, tremendous Allied advances across France and the fluid state of German defenses indicated the likelihood of another Airborne mission.

Twice the division was alerted and moved to departure airdromes to await the battle signal. Twice the division trudged to marshalling fields only to return to base camps. Swift-moving armor eliminated the necessity for both operations.

But the third operation wasn't a dry run. Its second combat mission -- Holland!

As part of the newly-formed First Allied A/B Army, Eagle soldiers were sent skyward toward German defenses in the land of wooden shoes and windmills. Again it was a sky dash over the English Channel, over flak towers, and down behind German lines.

The mission was to secure bridges and the main highway winding through the heart of Holland from Eindhoven to Arnhem to facilitate the advance of Gen. Sir Miles C. Dempsey's Second British Army over the flooded dike-controlled land.

Sept. 17 was the date for the 101st's second Airborne D-Day. The greatest Airborne fleet ever massed for an operation roared from U.K., spanned Channel waters. While the first planes spewed forth parachutists and gliders crash-landed on lowlands, planes and gliders transporting the division still were taking off from Britain air fields.

American paratroops of the 101st US Airborne receive a final briefing prior to setting out on the mission.

Flak met the invaders enroute, but the huge armada droned steadily on. Troop Carrier formations held firm despite fire. Pilots of burning planes struggled with controls as they flew to designated Drop Zones, disgorged their valuable cargoes of fighting men, and then plummeted earthward. Pilot heroism was commonplace, proved inspirational to Eagle sky fighters dropping well behind enemy lines.

Surprise was complete. There was little initial opposition from the Germans. Eagle veterans assembled quickly, then marched on their objectives.

Division missions called for the capture of Eindhoven and the seizure of bridges over canals and rivers at Vechel, St. Odenrode and Zon. To attain these objectives the division had to seize and hold a portion of the main highway extending over a 25 mile area. Commanders realized units would be strung out on both sides of the main arterial highway from Vechel to Eindhoven, that security in depth would be sacrificed.

Dropping near Vechel, the 501st Parachute Inf. Regt.,

commanded by Col. Howard R. Johnson, Washington, D.C., later killed in the campaign, pressed forward. Two hours later, Vechel was taken and bridges over the Willems Vaart Canal and the Aa River seized intact.

A sharp skirmish marked the speedy liberation of St. Odenrode by the 502nd Parachute Inf. under Col. John H. Michaelis, Lancaster, Pa. Co. H moved to take the highway bridge leading from Best. This small force was successful in its mission but driven back when Germans counter-attacked.

The fight for Best raged three days. At stake was a key communications route through which Germans could pour reinforcements. The enemy was deployed in strength at the Best bridge. The 502nd attacked again the second day to retrieve the bridge but was thrown back.

The bridge finally fell at 1800 the third day after one of the most bitter battles of the Netherlands campaign. The Airborne attack, supported by British armor, resulted in the destruction of fifteen 88s and the capture of 1056 Germans. More than 300 enemy dead littered the battlefield.

After landing, Col. Sink's 506th troopers moved toward Zon on the road to Eindhoven. Approaching Eagle soldiers saw Germans blow the bridge over the Wilhelmina Canal. Several men swam the Canal in the face of heavy German fire, established a bridgehead on the south bank. This action enabled the remainder of the regiment to cross.

Troopers whipped back the Germans as they drove towards Eindhoven five miles to the south. A flanking movement sealed the city's fate. The first major Dutch city to be liberated, Eindhoven, was in Airborne hands at 1300, Sept. 18.

On Sept. 23, Germans severed the main highway between Vechel and Uden. Simultaneously, they made a strong but unsuccessful bid to recapture Vechel.

With the highway cut, long caravans of trucks were halted along the narrow road leading from Eindhoven to Arnhem. All available division elements were rushed to the vicinity of Vechel where they were formed into a task force under Gen. McAuliffe.

Enemy penetrations were deep. German tanks and infantry moved within 500 yards of the vital bridges. Vicious fighting followed, but the Eagle defense held firm. The enemy was forced to withdraw toward Erp, and the highway was reopened.

Next day, a fresh German thrust cut the supply line between Vechel and St. Odenrode. Eagle soldiers combined with British tanks to smash German defenses and again reopen the road. Thereafter the thunderous roar of armor and supply trucks rolling up the highway continued uninterrupted.

Meanwhile, Gen. Taylor shuttled troops up and down both sides of the British Second Army's supply route to repulse German forces determined to sever Gen. Dempsey's lifeline.

Airborne troops, glidermen and paratroopers plugged gaps in the line with courage and M-1 rifles.

During the campaign in the canal-divided lowlands, hard-hitting Eagle paratroopers and glidermen again met a reorganized Normandy foe, the German 6th Parachute Regt. This crack German unit fared no better than before, sustaining heavy casualties which forced its early removal from the 101st sector.

Following this behind-the-enemy-lines "Airborne phase," the 101st moved to an area which soon became known to troops as the "Island." This strip of land was located between the Nederijn and Waal Rivers with Arnhem to the north, Nijmegen to the south.

Arrival of the Screaming Eagle on the Island marked the beginning of the end for Germany's 383rd Volksgrenadier Div. Taking over a quiet sector of the Island, the 101st prepared defensive positions.

Within 24 hours Germans struck from the west, slamming their 957th Regt. hard against the Airborne wall. Told it was opposing a handful of isolated Allied parachutists, hungry and without adequate weapons, the Nazi regiment attacked, confidently and swiftly.

The assault was absorbed by the depth of the 101st defense. The enemy was stunned at the savage reception accorded him by the "handful of Allied parachutists, hungry and without adequate weapons." Doggedly, the Germans drove -- into destruction. Soon, the 957th Regt. ceased to exist as a fighting tactical unit.

But the savage warfare wasn't over. Germans reorganized battered elements and the 958th Regt. arrived the next day to join its faltering fellow regiment. German artillery and armor supported a fresh attack. By nightfall, the Eagle battalion occupying Opheusden, focal point of the German effort for three days of fanatical fighting, withdrew to a defensive line east of the town.

Opheusden changed hands several times. Either attacking or withdrawing, skillful Eagle sky-fighters inflicted tremendous losses on the 363rd Div., now completely assembled with the 959th Inf. Regt., 363rd Arty. Regt. and its engineer and fusilier battalions in the fold. Airborne soldiers eventually captured the town, blasted retreating and thoroughly beaten Germans completely out of the Airborne sector.

Order of Battle records of enemy killed, wounded and captured provide mute testimony to the destruction of the German division. In its reorganized Volksgrenadier status, the once-proud 363rd Inf. Div. lasted exactly 10 days in the claws of the Screaming Eagles.

From then on, activity in Holland was limited to patrols. Highlighting the action was the work of an intelligence section patrol of the 501st Parachute Inf., led by Capt. Hugo S. Sims, Orangeburg. N.C., Regimental S-2.

The patrol crossed the Rhine in a rubber boat at night, and following a number of narrow escapes, reached an observation point on the Arnhem-Utrecht highway, eight miles behind enemy lines. After relaying information back to the division by radio, the patrol captured a number of German prisoners who gave additional data on units, emplacements and movement in the area.

Moving out next day, the six-man team nabbed a German truckload of SS troops, including a battalion commander. When the truck bogged down, patrol and PWs, now numbering 31, walked to the river, then crossed over to the American-held bank.

Early in November, the division was relieved in Holland and once again returned to a base camp, this time in France. Screaming Eagles paused for a breather. But it was brief because Eagle troops are not accustomed to resting. Since their activation they have been continually training, manoeuvring - - and now fighting.

CHAPTER 6

THE BRITISH FIRST AND SIXTH AIRBORNE DIVISIONS

This extract was originally published in 1945 in "By Air to Battle - The Official Account of the British First and Sixth Airborne Divisions", and descrbed the British experience of Operation Market-Garden.

Arnhem: The doorstep of Germany

By August 17th, 1944, the German armies, which four years and three months previously, had overrun so swiftly the whole land of France, were retreating even more swiftly towards their own country. More than a million men, British and American, bursting from their congested bridgeheads in Normandy, were sweeping, in a fury of controlled vengeance towards Germany. The Americans were soon to reach the Vosges and to link with the army of General Patch moving up from the Mediterranean ; The British composing the 21st Army Group, presently crossed the Siene and the Somme and did not halt till they were well beyond Brussells. To this great victory the contribution of airborne troops was considerable. Apart from the 6th Airborne Division, far to the south, in the vanguard of General Patch's invading army, were other airborne troops, tough sons of America, some of whom went to battle in British gliders flown by British pilots. Thirty-eight Horsas took them from a dusty in Rome to a still dustier one on Corsica, and thence to their landing zone near the little town of Frèjus on the French Riviera.

While these battles were being fought the tired veterans of 1st Airborne Division, now at full strength again, were waiting on

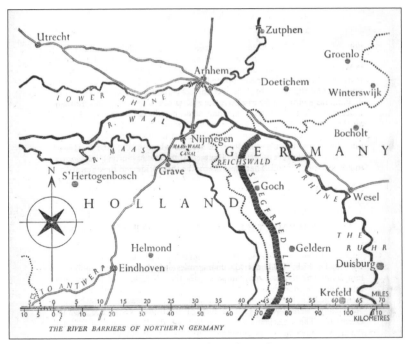

THE RIVER BARRIERS OF NORTHERN GERMANY

The river barriers of Northern Germany

the Berkshire Downs and in the windy spaces of Salisbury Plain, with an impatience they took small pains to conceal, to play their part in what might ultimately prove to be the final discomfiture of the enemy. At one time the period of waiting seemed likely to be long, for between June 6th and September 17th no less than sixteen airborne operations to support the Allied Expeditionary Force were planned, and all of them came to naught. The reason was simple. Time is needed to plan an airborne attack – not very much time, but enough to ensure that the aircraft and the men to be carried in them are ready and are accurately briefed ; for – and it is impossible to emphasise this too often – no airborne attack can succeed unless each man taking part in it knows exactly what to do and when to do it. On each of those sixteen occasions, before the moment for take-off arrived, the armies in the field had either reached or were threatening the proposed objective or the delay imposed by the enemy made the success of an airborne operation impossible. Action, therefore, by airborne forces was not necessary. So these fine troops had perforce to remain in chafing idleness till they were called upon to resolve a situation created by an advance which had exceeded all expectations, especially those of the Germans.

THE RIVER BARRIERS OF NORTHERN GERMANY

By the middle of September the British 2nd Army had broken through, crossed the Seine, advanced to Brussels and penetrated into Holland. To make this possible, the whole of its transport had been placed at the disposal of its leading Corps, and the other Corps had had perforce to remain more or less immobile. Even so, by the time the main body of the Corps had reached the Brussels-Antwerp line, the situation in regard to supply was already critical. That of the German forces opposed to them, however, was still more so. It may justly be described as chaotic. No organised resistance beyond the Seine had been possible, and it seemed that the remnants of the German 15th Army, which had been allotted the task of defending the Channel coast, were faced with but two alternatives. Either they could retreat into the fortified Channel ports of Boulogne, Calais, Dunkirk, and Ostend and there sustain themselves as long as possible, or they could try to find a way out into southern Belgium and Holland and, if successful, attempt to re-form behind the barriers which nature has there provided.

For a day or two something akin to panic seems to have prevailed among the German forces in the Dutch islands and on the mainland itself They had but one defensive position left before the Rhine and the frontiers of their country. It was provided by three rivers : the Meuse, which, when it crosses the Dutch frontier, becomes the Maas ; the Waal, which is the main branch of the German Rhine ; and the Lower Rhine. Had its difficulties of supply been overcome, there is little doubt that the 2nd Army might have pushed through and reached Germany. Yet this was impossible. The main lines of supply still ran from

Cherbourg and the artificial port of Arromanches, and large stocks of all sorts were held in dumps near these ports ; but road and rail communications between this base area and the front, over 250 miles away, were not equal to the task of supplying large forces which were still on the move and making heavy demands on stores of every kind. Thus were the Germans given breathing space, and they used it to the utmost.

THE RIVER BARRIERS OF GERMANY

The line of the Albert Canal was defended by what was left of the 15th Army, by detachments of the Hitler Jugend sent with all speed from Germany, and by such garrison troops as were available on the spot. The panic was ruthlessly checked by the adoption of the sternest measures, and as the days slipped by and the British armies made no further movement, the Germans consolidated their defence. Its most important section was that covered by the line of the three rivers just mentioned. Behind them was but a skeleton, for the Siegfried Line here peters out in the neighbourhood of the Reichswald. Between the end of this forest and the Waal at Nijmegen runs a ridge of ground which, though it is only 633 feet at its highest point above sea-level, constitutes the only range of hills in Holland. It is heavily wooded, but from the top it is possible to observe the country for a long distance in every direction. For many years this ridge had formed the favourite exercise ground for the Dutch Army, and the canal connecting the Maas with the Waal, and the Maas itself, running respectively along the western and southern sides of this hill, made it an ideal defensive position.

The Germans were quick to reinforce its natural strength by every possible means. There is no doubt that they feared an attack by airborne troops, and during the first fortnight of September they made all possible preparations to meet it. More and more anti-aircraft guns were brought up, and reconnaissance photographs showed each day some new position where work on digging them in had begun. Agents reported that the Dutch population, including twelve-year-old children, were being pressed into service to prepare a main defence line running along the Waal to the sea and a forward line following the Maas.

Field-Marshal Montgomery had two courses open to him. Either he could remain where he was, content with an advance which, in less than a month, had brought him to the threshold of Germany, or he could, by crossing the three river barriers in one fell swoop, seek to snatch the victor's final crown. He made the second and bolder decision, and he chose as his instrument as many of the airborne troops as could be assembled in time.

These consisted of three divisions, the 82nd and 101st, belonging to the American Army, tried troops whose mettle had been tested in the Cherbourg Peninsula, and the British 1st Airborne Division, whose valour in North Africa, in Sicily, and in southern Italy had earned for it a worthy reputation.

To them was given the task of forming a corridor of which the axis would be the Eindhoven-Veghel-Grave-Nijmegen-Arnhem road. Its formation would ensure a straight and swift advance to the gate of Germany. The bridges over the canals and rivers along the road, notably the nine-span steel bridge at Grave, that crossing the Maas-Waal Canal west of Nijmegen, the great single span steel road bridge over the Waal at Nijmegen and the bridge over the Lower Rhine at Arnhem were also to be seized.

The 101st American Division was to create that part of the corridor from Eindhoven to the outskirts of Grave ; the 82nd American Division was to establish its central section from Grave to Nijmegen and to capture the high ground south of Nijmegen overlooking the exits from the Reichswald; while the 1st British Airborne Division was to seize and hold the road bridge at Arnhem. These three divisions were, in fact, to form "a carpet of airborne troops " over which the 2nd Army might pour to break down the last barrier defending the Reich and thus gain direct access to the Ruhr.

A DAYLIGHT OPERATION IS PLANNED

The scale on which the operation was planned was larger than any which had previously been undertaken or contemplated. For the invasion of Normandy some 17,000 airborne troops had been used; for the capture of the three bridges many more must come into action. So great a number could not be transported in one lift. Moreover, the aircraft available were either Dakotas (C.47s) which are slow, unarmed and unarmoured transport aircraft not fitted with self-sealing tanks, or Stirlings, Halifaxes and Albemarles not designed to fly in daylight at a low height over hostile territory. For- and this was perhaps the most striking feature of the plan- the whole operation was to be carried out by the light of day. The Allied air forces were supreme in the air and attacks by fighters of the Luftwaffe were neither expected nor feared. The profusion of Spitfires, Thunderbolts, Mustangs, Typhoons and other fighters was so great that the protection they could give was rightly regarded as overwhelming.

There remained only the anti-aircraft defences of the enemy. As has been said, these were formidable and daily increasing. The dropping and landing zones were at extreme range and this meant that the transport and tug aircraft would have to follow the shortest possible route. The long, roaring columns would have to fly over the Dutch islands on which for the past four years the Germans had concentrated anti-aircraft batteries to prevent, if they could, the passage of day and night bombers on their way to the Ruhr.

Round the objectives themselves light flak was being concentrated in ever larger and larger quantities, Nevertheless the planners felt confident that the losses which might be incurred from anti-aircraft tire would not be so great as to imperil the operation. As it turned out, they were right, for it was only during the latter stages, when it became necessary to drop supplies to the men on the ground, that casualties became severe.

The task of the airborne troops was one with which most of

them were familiar-the capture of a bridge. This is an operation in which surprise must always play an important part. In this instance all three bridges were known to be prepared for demolition with charges built into the piers and exploding apparatus housed a short distance away. They were defended by dual-purpose guns which could be used both against aircraft and troops attacking on the ground. At Nijmegen the medieval citadel called Walkliof commanded the southern approach to the bridge and had been made into a strongpoint. Finally, and this was the most important consideration of all, the airborne army, for it was nothing less- could not remain long unsupported. Two days and nights were judged to be the maximum period during which it might be able to light on its own without the aid of the heavy artillery, the tanks, and all the other weapons at the disposal of armies on the ground.

In the event of the capture of the three bridges, could the leading Corps of the Second Army then push forward with sufficient speed to relieve the airborne forces in time 'I The task was difficult. Nevertheless, it was hoped and believed that it would be able to press on, provided always that the bridges were in Allied hands. Were it to be held up, however, elaborate arrangements were made for supplying the airborne troops from the air, though, even if all supplies fell in the right place and were collected without loss, those troops would still be without heavy artillery support against an enemy who before long would have at his disposal heavy and self-propelled guns. Yet all these risks were accepted in order to breach at one blow the last natural frontiers of Germany.

THE OBJECTIVES AT ARNHEM

To the 1st Airborne Division fell the honour of taking the bridge at Arnhem. Its commander, Major-General R. E. Urquhart, C.B., DSO., in conjunction with Lieutenant-General Browning in charge of the whole operation, drew up the simplest plan which would meet the circumstances. Even this, however, involved at least two, and, as it turned out, three lifts.

All the Division was to be used, together with the Polish Parachute Brigade. One factor governed the journey to the objective and the arrival there. The German airfield at Deelen and the town of Arnhem itself were very well protected by anti-aircraft guns. Situated as it was just to the north of Arnhem, comparatively slow-flying aircraft stood no chance if they approached too near to it in daytime. It was necessary therefore for the dropping and landing zones to be well beyond the range of the guns at Deelen.

Since the country round Arnhem is for the most part well wooded, the number of suitable open fields was not very great. Four, shown on the map as Y., S., L. and X., were eventually chosen. The first three lay immediately north of the railway running through Arnhem to Utrecht, the farthest of them, Y., being about eight miles from the bridge the capture of which was the object of the expedition. The fourth zone was south of the railway and somewhat larger than the others. A fifth, close to the city itself and near the small village of Warnsborn, was chosen as the place on which supplies were to be dropped after the landing. As will become apparent in due course, for the Royal Air Force it has become a place of glorious and tragic memory.

The troops at Urquhart's disposal comprised the 1st and 4th Parachute Brigades, the 1st Air Landing Brigade, the 21st Independent Parachute Company, the 1st Air Landing Reconnaissance Squadron, the 1st and 4th Parachute Squadrons and the 9th and 261st Field Companies of the Royal Engineers, the 1st Air Landing Light Regiment and the 1st and 2nd Anti-tank Batteries of the Royal Artillery, and detachments of the Royal Army Service Corps, the Royal Corps of Signals, the Royal Army Medical Corps and the Royal Electrical and Mechanical Engineers. The total number of officers and men who were airborne was 8,969, to whom must be added 1,126 glider pilots. The 1st Parachute Brigade consisted of the 1st, 2nd and 3rd Parachute Battalions, together with Headquarters and its defence platoon.

With them was the 16th Parachute Field Ambulance. The 10th, 11th and 15,6th Parachute Battalions composed the 4th Parachute Brigade, together with a defence platoon and the 133rd Parachute Field Ambulance. The 1st Air Landing Brigade was made up of the 2nd Battalion of the South Staffordshire Regiment, the 7th Battalion of the Kings Own Scottish Borderers, the 1st Battalion of the Border Regiment, and the 181st Field Ambulance.

Since it was impossible for all these troops to land on the same day, General Urquhart's plan was to put down immediately the 1st Parachute Brigade, the 1st Air Landing Brigade, and about half the available sappers and gunners and other divisional troops. The remainder would follow on the next day.

All were to fulfil a twofold task. First and foremost, the vital road bridge at Arnhem itself must be seized, together with, if possible, the pontoon bridge three-quarters of a mile downstream, and a railway bridge some two miles still farther west as the river flows. The seizure of the main bridge was to be carried out by the 1st Parachute Brigade, which would then form a small half-circle running through the town of Arnhem, its ends firmly based to east and west on the Lower Rhine. It was hoped that they would be able to accomplish this by nightfall on D Day. As soon as the remainder of the Division landed in the morning of the second day, they were to advance on Arnhem and construct a large perimeter running round the town itself, along the high ground to the west and north-west and across the flat fields to the east and south-east.

As soon as this second perimeter was formed, the 1st Parachute Brigade would come into reserve and be reinforced by the Polish Parachute Brigade, which would drop just south of the river near the main bridge. Some of them were to land in

gliders on the second day just north-east of the village of Wolf
hezen. Thus by the end of the second day, when relief from the
2nd Army could be expected, there would be an outer defence
round Arnhem and a solid reserve at the bridge itself. The outer
perimeter would enclose the zone at Warnsborn on which fresh
supplies would be dropped.

Such was the plan. Its success depended not only on the
bravery and dash of the troops-these could be taken for granted-
but on the inability of the Germans to react with sufficient
vigour, weight and speed. That the enemy would be surprised
seemed certain. How long he would take to recover from his
surprise was a factor far less easy to calculate. Therein lay the
risk, but it was one which Montgomery and Browning did not
hesitate to take, for the victor's palm falls to him who dares the
most.

The struggle for the crossings

At the outset all went well. The weather on Sunday, September
17th was good. At 10.15 in the morning, six officers and 180
men of the 21st Independent Parachute Company, under the
command of Major B. A. Wilson, took off in twelve Stirlings.
They were the Marker Force, and it was their duty to lay out the
aids and other indications for the guidance of the main body
following close behind them. They reached the dropping zones
without incident, only one aircraft being fired at. A few scattered
Germans were found on the ground and fifteen of them taken
prisoner. Two parachutists were hit during the descent, one in
his ammunition pouches, the other in his haversack. Neither was
hurt. In half an hour the marks were in position, and then the
first lift came in.

It was a fine sight to see the gliders carrying the 1st Air
Landing Brigade and Divisional Headquarters swoop down to
their appointed places, followed almost at once by the billowing
parachutes of the 1st Brigade swinging down in hundreds. The

drop and the glider landings were almost completely successful, ninety five per cent. of the troops reaching their rendezvous at the right place at the right time. The three battalions of parachutists and a parachute squadron of Royal Engineers forming the 1st Brigade under the command of Brigadier G. W. Lathbury, D.S.O., M.B.E., moved at once to their allotted task. It is their fortunes which must first be followed. The plan laid down for them was this : the 2nd Battalion, commanded by Lieutenant-Colonel J. D. Frost, D.S.O., M.C., a veteran of Bruneval, North Africa and Sicily, was to push on as fast as possible through the village of Heelsum and thence along the southern route, a road running close to the north bank of the Lower Rhine, until it reached the bridge, which it was to capture and hold. At the same time, the 3rd Parachute Battalion would be in the centre of the advance and move along the main Heelsum-Arnhem road to assist Frost's men by approaching the bridge from the north. The 1st Parachute Battalion was to remain with Brigade Headquarters in immediate reserve, ready to be used wherever and whenever the necessity arose.

As soon as the 2nd and 3rd Battalions had completed their immediate task, the 1st Battalion was to occupy the high ground just north of Arnhem.

To make assurance surer, most of the Air Landing Reconnaissance Squadron were to attempt a coup de main against the bridge. This, as it turned out, they were unable to do, for nearly all their transport failed to arrive.

The 2nd and 3rd Parachute Battalions, both of which had with them 2 troop of anti-tank guns and a detachment ofthe lst Parachute Squadron R.E., moved off punctually at three p.m. through well-wooded country. Let us first follow Frost and his 2nd Battalion. In Heelsum, where they arrived soon after leaving their dropping zone, they ambushed a number of Germarn vehicles and took about twenty prisoners. The Dutch inhabitants, who turned out in force, everyone wearing " some garment or

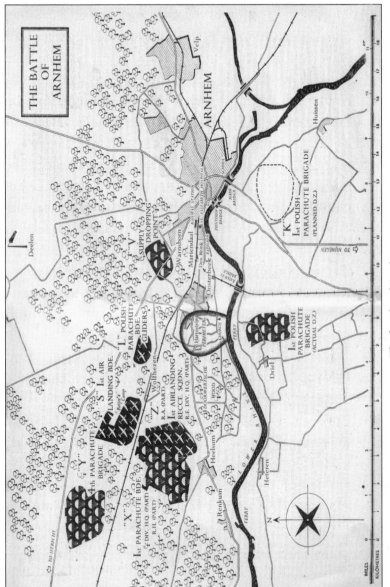

The battle of Arnhem

part of a garment coloured orange, some with favours, and some with orange armbands," said that there were but few Germans in Arnhem itself. The parachutists pushed on along the six miles of road which separated them from their goal, first encountering and overcoming opposition in Doorwerthsche Wood. On the way to the road bridge they had to pass to the north of the bridge carrying the railway over the river. Here trouble was caused by an armoured car and here, too, they suffered a disappointment. The railway bridge was blown just as Lieutenant Berry and a section of " C " Company reached it together with Captain E. O'Callaghan, M.C., and a number of the 9th Field Company R.E. Some of the men were actually on the bridge when it went up. " It seemed" said Corporal Roberts of the Royal Army Medical Corps, who was present, " to curl back on us, but no one was hurt."

COLLISION AT THE BRIDGE

The rest of the battalion pressed forward, and came under fire from some high wooded ground called Den Brink. This position was fiercely attacked by "B" Company, which took and held it at the cost of quite a few casualties. Meanwhile "A" Company skirted the position to the south, and moving close to the river, entered the town of Arnhem, where they met with small, scattered parties of Germans who were killed or captured. At eight o'clock, their eyes straining through the September dusk perceived the road bridge at last. Its half circle steel span was intact, and German transport was moving across it. The buildings commanding its northern end were immediately seized. A pill box which gave trouble was successfully deal with by a six pounder anti-tank gun and flame-throwers. Lieutenant Grayburn then attempted to rush across the bridge in order to capture its southern end. An anti aircraft gun and a German armoured car firing straight u the bridge brought this attack to naught, and Frost had to be content for the moment to hold on firmly to the northern end. He tried his best, however, to seize both ends and dispatched "B" Company, which had captured Den Brink, to cross the river lower downstream by means of a German pontoon bridge and by barge so as to outflank the southern defences of the road bridge. This they failed to do, for there were no barges and the pontoon bridge had been destroyed.

By the time Frost realized this, night had fallen ; but he held on. When dawn came, he found himself in command of a mixed force of between 600 and 700 men, with some six-pounder anti-tank guns. They were not long left in peace. About 11.30 in the morning a German column of six half-track vehicles, led by five armoured cars some fifteen to twenty yards apart, approached the bridge from the south. The armoured cars roared over it and went straight on into the town of Arnhem until they were tackled by the six-pounder anti-tank guns, which destroyed a number of them. The half-tracks were even less fortunate. When the leading vehicle arrived outside a school in which Lieutenant D. R. Simpson, M.C., R.E., with a number of Sappers, was installed, it ran into immediate trouble. Its driver and those of the rest were without the protection afforded by the armoured roofs, for these had been removed a few moments before by the six-pounders in action at the bridge itself. When, therefore, the half-tracks arrived at the school, their occupants fell an easy prey to the Sappers firing from its windows and from those of nearby houses.

The school itself stood in its own grounds and was of a square horseshoe shape, the ends of the two arms of the horseshoe being not above ten yards from the road. "I had men in one end," reported Simpson, "and Captain Mackay had some in the other. As the half-tracks came by, Corporal Simpson and Sapper Emery, whose conduct that day was outstanding, stood up and tired straight into the half-tracks with Sten and Bren guns. The range was about twenty yards." Five out of six of the half-tracks were knocked out almost at once, and created a block at the northern end of the bridge which made it impossible for any vehicles to pass. The driver of the sixth half-track, seeing the fate of the others, tried to bypass the obstacle created by the burning vehicles of his comrades, and pulled on to an asphalted path which ran under the windows of the school. His vehicle did not get far. It was hit, its crew climbed out, and sought the cover of the bushes, but were killed before reaching them."

After this unsuccessful attempt by the enemy to rush the bridge, he had recourse to continuous and heavy shell and mortar fire, which did a certain amount of damage to the houses in which Frost and his men were holding out. A heavy attack supported by several tanks and S.P. guns developed towards evening. It was driven back with the loss of one tank. Just as darkness fell, four of the houses held by the parachutists were set on fire and they had to seek other quarters.

THE 3RD BATTALION BREAKS INTO ARNHEM

So, for a night and a day, did the 2nd Battalion hold to the vital objective.

The fortunes or, to speak more truly, the misfortunes of the 3rd and 1st Parachute Battalions must now be considered. The 3rd Parachute Battalion under Lieutenant-Colonel J. A. C. Fitch had been engaged on their approach march to the bridge for less than an hour when, at a cross-roads about a mile and three-quarters south-east of Wolf hezen and half that distance from Oosterbeek, they ran into German infantry supported by two armoured cars. "B" Company, forming the advance guard, "were rather taken aback with this first sight of armour, because the six-pounder attached to them was facing the wrong way when the cars appeared and was knocked out when trying to face round." Nevertheless, a German staff car containing four staff officers was wiped out and the armoured cars dealt with, despite a lack of Flats. After this, "C" Company advanced through "B" towards the railway with orders to find any route they could by which to reach the bridge.

This was the last seen of them by the rest of the battalion. What happened to them was this. They moved down a small by-road and the platoons soon became separated. The leading one fought an action against a captured British jeep filled with Germans and pressed on, being presently caught up by the other two platoons, which had attacked an ammunition lorry and blown it up.

At dusk all three, now much reduced in numbers, reached the railway station at Arnhem and then moved on towards the bridge, through a town deserted save, says Sergeant Mason, "for two Dutch policemen .... We walked down a main street towards the bridge. Just before reaching it, a German car was blown up by a gammon bomb thrown by the leading platoon." A confused fight then ensued, and eventually what was left of the company entered the school close to the bridge and there joined the Sappers fighting beside Frost's 2nd Battalion. On the way to the school Private McKinnon, in the hope of finding food, entered a butcher's shop of which the owner, having no meat, gave him bread, wine and cheese. "He asked," says McKinnon, "if he could bring his daughter down to see me. She was twelve years old and she had one line of English to say, 'Many happy returns after your long stay away.'"

In the meanwhile the other companies of the battalion remained near the cross-roads a mile from Oosterbeek until two hours before dawn. Their advance then continued until they reached a point in Arnhem itself near the railway, where they came under heavy and persistent fire from eighty eight mm. guns. By that time the Headquarters Company, with which marched the mortars and machine-guns and a rifle company, were cut off from those in front, whose men presently got into houses and opened fire whenever possible on the German self-propelled guns and infantry. By one p.m they were under mortar fire, which continued for the next three hours, and at three o clock Lieutenant Burwash M C, with a party of men in a carrier arrived at Battalion Headquarters, having forced a way through the intervening Germans. They arrived somewhat exhausted, having run the gauntlet of several enemy posts ; but they had with them some much needed ammunition. This was distributed with difficulty, and it was decided to break out of the houses at four p.m. and push on at any cost to the bridge. Undeterred by their already heavy losses, the battalion did so, but was soon surrounded by an ever increasing number of the enemy and split into two groups which defended themselves with vigour through the night but could make no progress.

At dawn on the next day the 19th all that were still left reached the river bank and seized a large house called the Pavillion, but could not advance from it. There they were presently joined by such elements of the 1st Battalion as remained. "Casualties were being suffered at an ever increasing rate." The Germans too were in poor case. Those on the "promenade side" of the Pavilion "were very scared and wouldn't come down to the machine gun emplacements overlooking the road and fire their guns." Some, however, were made of sterner stuff notably the crew of a Spandau firing from a point near the Junction of the pontoon bridge and the road along the river's bank. They remained at their gun and prevented any further advance.

THE 1ST BATTALION FIGHTS THROUGH

The 1st Battalion had no better fortune. Under Lieutenant-Colonel D. T. Dobie, D.S.O., it moved off down the railway in an easterly direction following the 2nd and 3rd Battalions. "R" Company soon ran into opposition at a road junction north of the village of Wolfhezen and here a confused and desperate battle took place. The enemy were well posted on high wooded ground, and the battalion's casualties began to mount, until half "R" Company were killed or wounded. The remainder pressed on, and soon afterwards encountered five German tanks and fifteen half-track vehicles. "They could go no farther without coping with these and settled down to do so. Spasmodic but fierce fighting continued all that evening and at intervals throughout the night. " It was impossible," says Lieutenant Williams, "to make any headway. There were snipers in the woods on both sides. " What had happened was that the 2nd Battalion had preceded them along the same route earlier that afternoon, and the Germans, having been reinforced, had closed in behind them. There was very heavy opposition and there were snipers in practically every house. Individually the Germans were good, but as a body they were bad. "They weren't any good at tactics and made far more use of automatic weapons than rifles."

At first light on the 18th Lieutenant-Colonel Dobie received information that the 2nd Battalion was at the bridge and urgently needed reinforcements.

He decided to disengage his troops if he could, by-pass the enemy to the south, and move on towards the bridge. An attack by "S" Company on the left flank temporarily drove the enemy back with casualties, and the battalion pressed on a little farther, having by that time picked up the Headquarters Company of the 3rd Battalion. The fight presently shifted to some houses and a factory strongly held by the enemy near a railway bridge and a cross-roads at Mariendaal, a little suburb to the north-west of Arnhem. Here the battle raged all the morning, a first attack by "T" Company at nine o'clock being moderately successful, but a second attack on the factory failing because of the heavy fire of German twenty-mm. guns shooting northwards from the river bank. At this juncture Lieutenant-Colonel Thompson of the Light Regiment arrived and directed the fire of the seventy-five-mm. and the anti-tank guns, which were used with great effect against a pill-box in the factory. It received a direct hit and its fire was silenced. In all these engagements, or more accurately in this one long continuous struggle, heavy casualties were sustained by the enemy.

All that afternoon and evening the 1st Battalion tried to press forward, and did eventually reach the St. Elizabeth Hospital. By 6.30 p.m. its Commanding Officer was in touch with the 2nd Battalion, still holding the bridge and still urgently demanding reinforcements. By then his command was reduced to approximately a hundred men and there was hardly any ammunition. This deficit was presently remedied by the arrival of the remains of "R" Company, who had joined up with the 2nd South Staffordshire Regiment, and a plan was made to rush forward to the bridge at nine p.m. ' At eight p.m., however, the news came that the bridge had been overrun and the attack was put off. .

Thus did the three gallant battalions of the 1st Parachute Brigade struggle to fulfil their tasks in the first vital forty-eight hours. The 2nd succeeded, for it reached and held the bridge though the conditions in which it did so increased in difficulty with every hour. The other two made determined but mostly vain efforts to reach their hard-pressed comrades ; but the main design on which the success of the operation principally depended had not been achieved. The semicircle round the bridge had not been formed and did not exist.

"Would you like to throw a bomb, sir? "

The Divisional General was an eye-witness of this fighting and himself took part in it. On landing, he made a rapid tour of his brigades and presently reached the 1st, under Brigadier Lathbury, who was with the 3rd Battalion. By then the Germans had woken up and there was considerable fire from snipers and mortars. This caused many casualties among the 3rd Battalion, and the position was such that at dusk the Major-General and the Brigadier came to the conclusion that to return to Brigade Headquarters was out of the question. They therefore remained with the 3rd Battalion, whose Headquarters had been established near a cross-roads on the main Arnhem-Heelsum road, half a mile from the suburb of Hartestein. The two men spent the night in a small house and moved off about four o'clock in the morning.

By then Urquhart's jeep had been hit and the driver knocked out. His wireless, too, was not working, and he was therefore out of touch with everyone except the troops in the immediate neighbourhood. He and the Brigadier continued to push forward into Arnhem in the wake of the 3rd Battalion in conditions which became increasingly difficult. The mortar fire was by then heavy and made it necessary to take cover in the houses. "Self propelled guns," reports the Major-General, "cruised up and down the street shooting at us and getting very aggressive." .

Between four and five in the afternoon the small party--it consisted of the Divisional Commander, Captain W. A. Taylor, Brigadier Lathbury and a subaltern-decided to move out of the house in which they had been compelled to remain for some hours. .To cover their advance smoke bombs were used. The demeanour of the senior officers was very polite. The Brigadier said to the Major-General, "Would you like to throw a bomb, sir?" He answered, "Oh, no, you'd be much better at it than I am."

Under cover of this smoke they went through some back gardens and into a street, across the end of which they ran till they reached the next street.

Here the Brigadier was hit in the back and fell to the pavement. General Urquhart and Captain Taylor picked him up and carried him into a house, where they stowed him in the cellar. While they were doing so, a German appeared at the window and Urquhart dispatched him with his revolver.

It is seldom in modern war that the Commander of a Division has an opportunity to fight the enemy at such close quarters. Leaving the Brigadier, at his urgent request, for he was partly paralysed and could not walk, they went to another house where they remained for the rest of the evening and the next night. For many hours, such were the circumstances of this peculiar battle, the Commander of the force had been unable to exercise more influence upon it than that which could be brought to bear by any private soldier engaged in it. Through the night they waited in the loft, discouraged from making an attempt to quit their-quarters by a self-propelled gun which "came along the road and parked itself in front of our door." In the early morning of the l9th they escaped during a lull, and Urquhart, leaping into a passing jeep, reached Hartestein and was at last able to resume control.

While he had been thus lost, his place had been taken by Brigadier P. H. W. Hicks, D.S.O., MC., whose every effort was directed towards concentrating as many men as possible in the area of the vital bridge. How the 1st Parachute Brigade endeavoured to seize and hold it has already been told. Their efforts were later seconded by "B" and "D" Companies of the 2nd Battalion of the South Staffordshire Regiment under the command of Colonel W. D. McCardie. They had landed by gliders at the Reijer's Camp landing zone. The remainder of the Battalion was to come in with the second lift.

After a sharp engagement near Mariendaal to the immediate west of Arnhem, the two companies, with a detachment of the 9th Field Company R.E., eventually got through and entered the town, one at about seven in the evening of the 18th, the other about midnight. There they made contact with what remained of the 1st and 3rd Parachute Battalions.

The gliders arrive on schedule The remainder of the first lift, consisting of the 1st Battalion of the Border Regiment and the 7th Battalion of the King`s Own Scottish Borderers, arrived on schedule. It was their duty to seize and hold the landing grounds and dropping zones, so that the second lift, due to land on the next day, might do so in safety. Lieutenant-Colonel R. Payton-Reid, commanding the Borderers, paints a dry picture of the flight and the arrival. "We started off," he says, "in a certain amount of low mist, which caused some of the gliders to release over England. However, when we got over the Channel it was bright and clear. We had a good trip, not bumpy. Three of my gliders went down in the sea. They were all picked up in fifteen minutes by the Air Sea Rescue Service. It was interesting to see the Dutch islands all flooded completely, except for a few buildings sticking up out of the water. There was no flak.

"The first glider came down at 1.30 and we all moved off at three o'clock. Everything was unloaded by then. We had no local help. There were one or two crashed gliders. We couldn't get out the motor bikes and one anti-tank gun. A lot of the gliders' undercarriages came up through the bottom because we landed on very soft ground. Eight gliders didn't arrive, otherwise we were complete, just over 700 men and forty officers. The battalion landed to the tune of its regimental march, 'The Blue Bonnets over the Border,' played by a piper who continued to march up and down the rendezvous till all the men had reached it."

Throughout the afternoon and the night the Borderers held the dropping zones, being thrice unsuccessfully attacked by the Germans.

What happened to the Border Regiment covering the dropping zones to the south - those to the north were held by the Borderers - was very similar. They suffered to a certain degree from mortar fire, which by the end of the 18th had destroyed all the vehicles belonging to "B" Company.

Whether the course of the battle in the first twenty-four hours would have been changed, had it been possible for Major-General Urquhart to use these two Battalions of the Air Landing Brigade to reinforce the hard-pressed 1st Parachute Brigade, must at present remain a matter of conjecture. The tenacious resistance of the Germans on the high ground west and north of Arnhem proved too strong for the comparatively lightly armed parachute battalions to overcome. Had more troops been thrown into the battle success might well have been achieved, but it was precisely this possibility which was denied to Urquhart. At any cost he had to hold the landing zone so that his reinforcements might be able to land without incurring prohibitive casualties. At the crucial moment, therefore, on the afternoon that September Sunday, he lacked just that added punch which might have knocked down the German guard. Had the whole Division been carried in one lift, the Border Regiment and the Borderers would not have had to play a comparatively static role in the first and all- important twenty-for hours, nor would the South Staffords have had to go into action with on half their strength.

The impossibility of arranging for all units to arrive together was or reason why the 1st Airborne Division failed to hold the crossings of the Lowe Rhine. Another was also to become apparent in the first twenty-four hours. The plan provided for the arrival of the second lift containing the balance of the Division at latest by ten in the morning of Monday, the 18th. That day broke fine and clear over Arnhem, and the spirits of the men fighting in its streets and in the woods around its trim houses were uplifted when they saw the bright sun and the clear sky. Major Wilson was soon busy putting out more markers, for he and his men heard the sound of aircraft approaching. They had been told that any they might see or hear would be friendly ; but, as they were completing their task, they looked up and saw a numb of Messerschmitt 109s diving upon them. They leapt hastily for cover. The minutes began to go by, and then the hours, and still the second lift did not appear, for on this side of the Channel cloud and foggy conditions prevented combinations from taking off till after midday. It was not until between three and four in the afternoon that they arrived in the landing area. This delay of several vital hours still further complicated a situation which was becoming increasingly difficult.

THE SECOND LIFT COMES IN

The arrival of the second lift was accomplished with but few casualties. They had left in "very filthy weather indeed, low cloud and rain," but after a while it improved and, says Major R. Cain of the South Staffords, who was soon to win a Victoria Cross, "a little while after mid-Channel I saw the coastline of Holland in front. It was a buff-fawny colour, with white and grey streaks .... The next thing I recognised was the Rhine. Then we got flak puffs all round us and bits of tracer. I got the fellows strapped in. Geary, the glider pilot ... put her into a dive approach. It seemed to be about treetop level when he pulled her out straight and shouted 'Hold tight' and we landed in a ploughed field .... We got out and took up all-round protective positions .... All the area was divided up into square fields with little tree-lined earth roads dividing them. It was very neat and very square. The trees were elms. I could hear very little firing and what there was a long way off. There was no other activity."

The enemy were, however, more active than on the first day. It was under heavy fire that Lance-Sergeant Maddocks of the South Staffords, for example, had to saw off the tail of his glider in order to unload a Vickers gun, and Flight-Sergeant Carter, one of twenty-five instructors from the Parachute Training School who that day flew with some of their erstwhile pupils, found himself dispatching an officer, a sergeant-major and sixteen men of the 10th Parachute Battalion from a burning Dakota twenty miles or more from the dropping zone. This task he accomplished without loss, and himself jumped with the American crew whose' pilot, Lieutenant Tucker, remained at the controls to the last possible moment and thus ensured a safe drop.

Carter joined the advanced elements of the leading Corps of the Second Army Corps and was back at his task of instructing four days later.

Generally speaking, however, the second lift arrived without undue difficulty. A few gliders did not. One, carrying Lieutenant A. T. Turrell and his men, was shot down between Nijmegen and Arnhem but succeeded in making a good landing. Thirty Dutchmen helped to unload the glider, among them a girl who to do so abandoned her search for a green parachute among those lying about. She wanted it, she said, to make a dress of that colour. Under the guidance of a Dutch priest and a local official the party set oh" for the Division, who were the other side, of the Rhine. On the Way they met with six Germans whom they disarmed and locked in the local gaol, after first making them take off their uniforms and put on civilian clothes.

All eventually reached the neighbourhood of Arnhem by crossing the Lower Rhine in a ferry.

Once the second lift was down, Brigadier Hicks, still in command of the Division in the continued absence of the Major-General, decided at any cost to reinforce those holding the bridge. He had some knowledge of what was happening from the Dutch inhabitants of Arnhem, who showed the greatest courage and resolution in keeping him informed. The telephone exchange had been taken over by members of the Resistance Movement, who passed messages whenever possible. A tall, cadaverous Dutchman volunteered, provided he could be fitted out with a uniform, to take a jeep to the bridge with ammunition. The 1st and 3rd Battalions of the 1st Parachute Brigade were disintegrating in the streets of Arnhem ; they must be reinforced. In order to do so, Hicks instructed the 2nd South Staffords to move along the road beside the river, while the 11th Parachute Battalion, forming part of the 4th Parachute Brigade which had just landed, was to take the northern route so as to effect the same object. Neither the Parachute Battalion nor the South Staffords could get farther than the St. Elizabeth Hospital and a building called the Monastery, both some distance from the bridge, though they started with comparative ease.

"We moved off in the proper order of march," says Major

Cain, "and I remember checking several men as they went past for things like not having their bayonets fixed. It was so like an exercise that I did this automatically."

They passed through the suburb of Wolf hezen, badly smashed by the medium bombers of the 2nd Tactical Air Force two nights before, and then found themselves in an outer suburb of "extremely attractive houses gaily painted in every sort of colour. They were bright colours, but somehow they looked right. These houses were set back in the woods and were without the railings and fences round the gardens that we have in England. The people . . . stood in the road, greeting us. They offered us water and apples, which I think was all they had. The street we went down might have been the outskirts of any English town, but it was cleaner. There were one or two factories. The houses stood in rows but were not detached. I saw our troops talking to an attractive blonde through a window. We were very confident, then."

The South Staffords ran into heavy fire on the western outskirts of Arnhem and were eventually challenged near the junction of the road with the railway running up from Nijmegen. Night had long since fallen, for they had taken thirteen hours to cover three miles ; but their challenger, who was a glider pilot, cheered them by saying that they were now only two miles from the bridge ; he added, however, that the road was under machine-gun fire.

At a conference between the Commanders of the reinforcing Battalions and Lieutenant-Colonel O. Dobie, D.S.O., commanding the remnants of the 1st and 3rd Parachute Battalions still fighting in Arnhem, it was decided to continue the advance at first light, the South Staffords on the left, the parachute troops on the right, nearest the river.

Soon they reached the St, Elizabeth Hospital, marked by "a statue of a female wearing a crown and flowing robes, set in the wall," and a large Geneva flag, and the leading platoons of the

South Staffords pushed on 400 yards farther east and by 6.30 a.m. had captured the Monastery.

To advance farther was impossible, for the pressure of the enemy was increasing every moment. So close indeed were the Germans that to use mortars was very difficult: "they were shooting almost straight up in the air." The attackers, now thrown on the defensive, were without anti-tank guns, which could not be brought up because of the heavy fire on the road behind. There were, however, a number of Piats available.

To advance further was impossible, for the pressure of the enemy was increasing every moment. So close indeed were the Germans that to use mortars was very difficult : "they were shooting almost straight up in the air." The attackers, now thrown on the defensive, were without anti-tank guns, which could not be brought up because of heavy fire on the road behind. There were, however, a number of Piats available.

For three hours the German attacks were beaten off, largely by the efforts of Lieutenant Georges Dupenois, Major Buchanan and Major Cain. "When a tank appeared we got four Brens firing on it with tracers. That shut its lid up, because the commander couldn't stand up in the turret. As soon as we'd let off a Piat at it, we'd move back and then the German shells would explode below us." About 11.30 in the morning the ammunition for the Piats gave out, the position was overrun, and what remained of the heroic South Staffords withdrew to a wooded dell just west of the Monastery.

It became a shambles. The German tanks came up and fired right into it, causing heavy casualties. "We could hear the call 'Stretcher bearer' all the time. There was no effective fire going back against these beasts because we had no ammunition."

Despite its heavy losses the 1st Parachute Battalion still had fight in it. It sought to share in the advance, and Major Perrin-Brown led "T" Company, the parachute war cry "Whoa, Mohammed!" bursting from their throats, in a bayonet charge which reduced their strength to eight men. A little later Major Timothy led "R" Company in a similar charge and fought on till only six were left. Their pertinacity had brought them to within a thousand yards of the bridge, and they could do no more. The few left, nearly all wounded, presently fell with their Colonel into the enemy's hands.

FIGHTING TO ESTABLISH AN OUTER PERIMETER

While these efforts were being made to reinforce Frost at the bridge, the rest of the Air Landing Brigade and the 4th Parachute Brigade, which had come in with the second lift, were seeking to establish the outer perimeter and thus fulfil the second part of the original plan. To do so the 4th Parachute Brigade, under Brigadier J. W. Hackett, D.S.O., M.B.E., M.C., assaulted the high ground which had proved such a grim obstacle to its original attackers, the 1st Brigade. They had no better success, for by now the Germans had completely recovered from the initial surprise and, what was worse, had been reinforced. The arrival of the second lift in the afternoon instead of the morning had given the enemy six hours' respite, and he had taken all possible advantage of it.

Nor were the Border Regiment and the King's Own Scottish Borderers north of the railway more successful. The second had lost a certain number of men holding the dropping and landing zones ; but so effectively had they accomplished their task that the casualties among the 4th Parachute Brigade on landing were very small. At seven o'clock in the evening the Borderers moved forward to occupy the positions allotted to them in the high ground north-west of Arnhem. They reached them with difficulty in the middle of the night and held on the next day, being joined in the afternoon by a number of Poles who had landed in gliders near Wolf hezen and suffered very heavily in doing so.

While the Commanding Officer of the Borderers was conferring with the Brigadier at Brigade Headquarters, the

Germans launched an attack. On returning, he says, "I found the hell of a battle going on." He had just been ordered to withdraw his battalion south of the railway to avoid being taken in the rear, but, before he could do so, he had to beat off this attack. "This we did successfully," he reports, "Major Cochran, who was afterwards killed, killing twenty of the enemy, and Drum-Major Tate the same number. . . All the Boches who weren't killed turned and went back into the woods, so I took the opportunity of going south." Eventually the battalion, now reduced to fewer than 300 men, got into a position in two large houses near a small wood just south of the railway.

The Border Regiment were farther to the east, and "B" Company, in the village of Renkum, held out successfully against heavy attacks. "We got ourselves into houses and a factory," says Lieutenant Skilton, and in the morning the Germans started walking round the town. We waited till they got together in the main street into a number of nice little groups. Then we opened fire and killed thirty-five at very short range. That rather upset them, but they returned to the attack, and our position was very heavily shelled with mortars and self-propelled guns, whose fire destroyed most of buildings we were in, and all our transport." "D" Company was equally tenacious and beat off attack after attack launched against the landing it was defending throughout a period of thirty-six hours.

Major Wilson's independent Parachute Company and the glider pilots also shared in this heavy fighting. Having laid out the markers for second lift, the Independent Company then met with snipers from an S.S. Battalion and immediately attacked them. Very soon "the Germans in their sniper's suits crawled out of their slits and grovelled on the ground begging for mercy. They were terrified to see men wearing red berets and had to be violently persuaded to their feet." The assaults of the enemy continued however, especially during the night and on the morning of the third and "whenever the Germans attacked they all shouted to each other, it being obviously part of the drill, and above their shouts could be heard the voices of the N.C.Os. cursing and swearing and urging them on to battle. This shouting sounded eerie in the woods."

The glider pilots, after having safely brought the troops to the battle, now as heavily engaged as their passengers. Those who had flown in the first lift helped to hold the landing zones and then, when the second lift had come in, fought side by side with the King's Own Scottish Borderers and eventually formed part of the defence of Divisional Headquarters, established at Hartestein. They were soon heavily engaged, and with them were Troops of the 4th Parachute Squadron R.E., one of whose officers, Captain H. F. Brown, earned a Military Cross for the manner in which he lead the sappers fighting as infantry. Thus after two and a half days of bitter, unceasing strife, the first phase ended. The northern end of the bridge been taken and was still in our hands ; but the rest of the design had awry.

A CONFUSED AND BITTER STRUGGLE

That this was so had been realized by Major-General Urquhart who, soon as he had escaped from the house on the outskirts of Arnhem, had taken over command once more. Now he was faced with a difficult and urgent decision. Was it still possible to carry out all or part or none of the plan ? The Air Landing Brigade had established itself more or less in position originally chosen, west and south-west of Arnhem. For sixty hours the 1st Parachute Brigade had been heavily involved in the town and the position of its battalions was very obscure except that, as far as was known Frost and his men were still at the bridge. The 4th Parachute Brigade, which was to hold that part of the perimeter comprising the northern approaches to Arnhem had been unable to capture their positions. How could what remained of it best be used ?

Urquhart soon decided that it was quite out of the question to attempt to put it north of the railway, in other words to create that outer perimeter which should include the town within its embrace. On the afternoon third day, therefore, the Brigade was ordered to disengage and to move of the railway so as to occupy, if possible, the high ground between Oosterbeek and the town ; but even this task proved impossible. With staccato clarity the diary of the 156th Parachute Battalion, one of its units, tells why. On the day before, in twenty-four hours two of its companies, striving to make headway, had been cut to pieces in the woods just north of the railway.

"0830 hours. ' A ' Company put in an attack on the line of defence on the road running from Arnhem to Utrecht. The company met very heavy opposition including S.P. guns and armoured cars after suffering heavy casualties, including all officers. "0900 hours. ' B ' Company put in an attack on the same line moving round the north of 'A' Company and met with the same heavy opposition. Its commander was wounded and heavy casualties were sustained."

By the afternoon of September 19th, therefore, the battalion was already gravely reduced in numbers, when "orders were received from Headquarters to move to the area of the hotel at Wolfhezen in fifteen minutes' time. Owing to the speed of this move and the fact that the enemy were attacking, the battalion got divided and "S" Company and half of "B" and "C" Companies moved along the north side of the railway. They were attacked and overrun during the night, and except for the Quartermaster and six men, have not been heard of or seen since."

Sergeant T. C. Bentley of the 10th Parachute Battalion, equally involved in this action, is more explicit. "We were given orders," he says, " to leave the wood. It was every man for himself, for by then we were all split up. The top of the wood was occupied by fifty or sixty Germans .... Sergeant Sunley and Sergeant Houghton were terrific. We ran across a playing field and found several men showing yellow triangles. We understood that they were Poles .... We had by then lost about two-thirds, but the men were still in good heart though they had no more support weapons."

What happened to the 10th and 156th Parachute Battalions is typical of the fate suffered by the rest of the Brigade. There was no respite given or demanded. Captain L. E. Queripel of the 10th Parachute Battalion was especially conspicuous. After carrying a wounded sergeant to cover under heavy fire, he was himself hit in the face but, undeterred, continued to lead his men. A strong-point composed of a captured British anti-tank gun and two machine-guns was a cause of trouble and casualties. Captain Queripel attacked it alone, killed its occupants, and recaptured the gun. Later that day he was again wounded, but insisted on covering the withdrawal of his men from a position which had been untenable for several hours but had none the less been held. In so doing he exhausted the ammunition of his automatic pistol and threw every grenade he could find at the enemy. He did not rejoin his men and was not seen again. For these deeds he was awarded the Victoria Cross.

Captain R. Temple was at Brigade Headquarters, which, after losing all its transport, had taken to a hollow south of the railway. "We spent," he says, "most of the day there being attacked all the time .... At one stage we thought the Germans wanted to surrender, and they thought that we did. . . . By Wednesday evening the strength of the Brigade was about 250. We were practically out of ammunition and the Germans were still attacking."

Eventually what remained of the Brigade reached the area of Divisional Headquarters ; but by then it was not more than 150 strong, and it was obvious that the task given it was beyond its strength. Urquhart, therefore, with great reluctance, was forced to take a decision which meant the abandonment of all the troops near the bridge, the seizure of which had been the main object of the operation. The virtual destruction of the 4th Parachute Brigade in the woods north and north-west of Arnhem, the virtual disappearance of the 1st Parachute Brigade in the town itself, and the heavy losses sustained by the Air Landing Brigade left him, indeed, no choice.

He decided to form a perimeter round the suburb of Oosterbeek and there hold out until the long expected relief from the 2nd Army arrived, using for this purpose the remains of the 4th Brigade together with any other troops available.

STRANGE EPISODES OF THE BATTLE

The accounts which have come to hand of the fierce lighting of those first days, though confused and incomplete, for many who took part in them are dead and many were captured, show the indomitable spirit of these airborne troops, their skill and high heart, and their strange cheerfulness in conditions of the most adverse kind. At one point the Germans brought up a loudspeaker which first played jazz music and then urged the "Gentlemen of the 1st Airborne Division to remember your wives and sweethearts at home." It ended by enumerating a list of the more important officers alleged to be already prisoners, and by promising a heavy attack by an entire Panzer Division. "This monologue," says Captain H. F. Brown, M.C., R.E., "was not allowed to be heard for long, for it was greeted by abuse, catcalls, whistles and occasional bursts from a Bren gun. We all thought it was a great joke." A Piat being fired in the direction of the loudspeaker, "there was a big bang and it stopped."

Major Gordon Sherriff of the King's Own Scottish Borderers, going round the posts with his Colonel, ran into someone who spoke German. The first to recover from his surprise was the Major who, though suffering from a wound, tackled the man with his bare hands and killed him. The Colonel whom he accompanied on that occasion was Payton-Reid, whose stout exploits and those of his battalion have already been mentioned.

An officer of the South Staffords left Arnhem for the slightly less unhealthy neighbourhood of Oosterbeek by rolling away from a tank which had stopped within Fifty yards of him. Its commander was "standing up as bold as anything in the turret, wearing black gloves and with hand held glasses in his hand " ; but he failed to see the British officer, who rolled over and over slowly away from the trench in which he had been sitting till he reached a wall. This he climbed, and then fell twenty feet into the courtyard of the hospital beyond and "quietly passed out for ten minutes. Then I got up and moved through the back of the hospital and so out of Arnhem. "

For the first few days, and until reinforcements reached the area, the confusion in the enemy's ranks caused by the arrival of the parachutists was very great. Individual Germans did not know what was happening, or even that any airborne attack had been made. Having set off that morning on his rounds to pay the troops, a German field cashier, for example, drove in a sidecar into the position of the Independent Parachute Company with a bag full of Reichsmark notes, while a German lorry driver, wearing a Dutch farmer's smock, took his vehicle past another of our posts. As he had forgotten to take off his steel helmet he did not get by ; the truck was fired on and, since it contained ammunition, exploded.

Then there was the episode of the Piat, the company cook and the German tank. A hospital had been established in a large house in a street where fighting was fierce and continuous, the enemy being in some of the houses and our men in others including one next door to the hospital. The German commander sent its garrison a message by the regimental doctor to the effect that, if they did not evacuate the house, he would blow them to pieces with his tanks, of which he had three. The British officer in command replied that he was prepared to move if the German promised not to enter the hospital.

At the same time he told his company cook to slip out by the back door and fire on the leading German tank with a Piat. The cook, Dixon by name, knew more of pots and pans than of Piats, but his first shot hit the back of the tank and exploded the ammunition it carried. The Germans at once retreated and ceased to menace the hospital. Episodes such as these stand out from the dull background of unceasing danger, utter lack of sleep and slow torment from hunger and thirst. All these and more were steadfastly endured. Already the 2nd Army was two days overdue and no relief was in sight ; yet the Division held on.

THE VALIANT DEFENDERS OF THE BRIDGE

Before recounting the last stand round the village of Oosterbeek, We must return to the bridge and the men who had captured it by nightfall of the first day, and who still held on with grim tenacity long after all hopes of relief or reinforcement had vanished. The destruction of the German armoured cars and half-track vehicles which sought to cross the bridge and enter Arnhem on the morning of the 18th showed the enemy that the Parachutists were strongly established and in force. He therefore began to mortar the houses and positions on or near the bridge ; these were held by the 2nd Battalion and remnants of the 3rd, supported by elements of the Headquarters of the 1st Parachute Brigade, of the Royal Engineers, the R.A.M.C. and R.A.S.C., of the Light Regiment of Artillery and one troop of anti-tank guns. This mortar fire continued as long as there were any airborne troops in the area.

In the afternoon of the 18th an enemy attack succeeded in driving some of the Brigade defence platoon out of their houses, but the two German tanks leading it were eventually knocked out, one by a six-pounder, the other by a Piat ; and just before dark, four houses were set on fire and their garrisons had therefore to leave them. All through that day there had been many rumours that the 1st and 3rd Battalions would arrive with much needed reinforcements, but by late afternoon no one had appeared and hope died, to be revived, however, by the news that the South Staffordshires and the 11th Parachute Battalion were fighting their way towards the bridge.

In an endeavour to deal with Frost and his men before their arrival, the Germans, about sunset, formed up for an infantry attack but were forestalled by the parachutists. Shouting their battle-cry, "Whoa, Mohammed!" they charged the enemy with the bayonet and the Germans fled.

After an uneasy night with many alarums and excursions the captors of the bridge prepared at dawn on the 19th to deal with further counter-attacks. These did not develop immediately, for at first the enemy contented himself with heavy mortaring and shelling, the shells being fired by tanks which had crept up to a position close to the river bank. This fire lasted throughout the morning until Captain A. Frank dealt with the tanks by means of Piats, scoring three direct hits but using all the remaining ammunition.

The German tanks limped away, and about this time Lieutenant McDerment recaptured a house from which he and his platoon had been driven. The battle swayed this way and that ; but in general, despite the fierce efforts of the enemy, the defenders of the bridge held on and did not falter, not even when a Tiger tank moved down the road just before dark and pumped shells into each house in turn. The casualties it caused included Father Egan, MC., who had served from the outset with the Brigade, and Major A.D. Tatham-Warter, both of whom were wounded but remained in action. The method used by the defence was to stalk the tanks by moving from room to room through the houses, knocking holes in the partition walls in order to do so, and thus getting close enough to fire a Piat or throw a gammon bomb.

It was in this way that Lieutenant Simpson knocked out a tank close to the house in which he was posted. Its crew got out and "crept along the wall till they came to a halt beneath the window where I was crouching. I dropped a grenade on them and that was that. I held it for two seconds before I let it drop."

In the morning of the next day Frost, who was in command of the whole force, was badly wounded and the active defence was taken over by Major C. F. H. Gough, M.C., commanding the Reconnaissance Squadron, though Frost continued to do all he could to bear a share in the fighting. To report his presence and the situation at the bridge, Gough spoke to the Divisional Commander, using not wireless, for all the sets were out of order, but the Arnhem telephone system. The exchange was held and operated by Dutch patriots, but to make sure that any German who might be listening in would not be able to identify him, Gough referred to himself throughout as "the man who goes in for funny weapons."

THE FINAL STAND AT THE BRIDGE

By midnight the defence was "greatly weakened." The 2nd Battalion, commanded first by Major Wallis and, after his death, by Major Tatham-Warter, whose conduct was exemplary even amid so much gallantry, had suffered heavy casualties ; so had its supporting troops, among whom must be numbered the signallers fighting as infantrymen under Captain B. Briggs.

Ammunition was running short, and the key house commanding the north end of the bridge had been burnt down. The Germans posted in houses farther back nearer the town, though making no attempt to infiltrate, kept the whole area of the defence under more or less continuous small arms and automatic fire. The number of wounded had now reached serious proportions. They were lying in the cellars of a house, attended by two Royal Army Medical Corps doctors, Captains J. Logan, D.S.O., and D. Wright, M.C., who did particularly tine work in dreadful conditions and remained with them to the end. The order to surrender the wounded was given by Colonel Frost after the house had been set on fire. Wednesday, September 20th, brought no relief. By then the Force had been burnt out of its original positions on or near the bridge and was lighting in the ruins close to and beneath it. Presently German tanks were able to move across the bridge from north to south, for the six-pounders, sighted to cover it, were under small arms fire and could not be manned. Aircraft also played a part in the German attacks, and a Messerschmitt 109, diving on the position, hit the steeple of a nearby church and crashed. Nevertheless, the defence was still maintained and hopes were still high, for news had been received that the 2nd Army would attack the south end of the bridge that afternoon at five p.m.

By now those of the defenders who were not beneath the bridge were holding slit trenches hastily dug in the gardens of the houses from which they had been driven by fire. The spirit of the defence is best exemplified by the following wireless dialogue which was overheard.

Captain Briggs : The position is untenable. Can I have permission to withdraw ?

Frost : If it is untenable you may withdraw to your original position.

Captain Briggs : Everything is comfortable. I am now going in with bayonets and grenades.

The final stand was made, first in a warehouse, and then underneath the bridge, the total number still capable of fighting being about 110 men and five or six officers. The position was shelled by a German tank and armoured car, but they were unable to hit that part of the underside of the bridge where the defence was holding out. It was at this juncture that Lieutenant Grayburn, whose valour earned him a Victoria Cross which he did not live to receive, led a series of counter-attacks, in one of which Germans laying charges to blow the bridge were killed and the charges torn out. Every time a patrol went out it suffered casualties, and with each hour the situation became more and more hopeless. There was no more ammunition, there had been no food for a long time, and hardly a man but was wounded. The very ground on which the defenders stood or crouched was constantly seared by flames from the burning houses about it, and no man could remain there and live.

So in the end the gallant remnant were dispersed or captured.

The battle of the perimeter

While this resolute and increasingly desperate stand was being made at the bridge, the fighting had veered from Arnhem itself to the village of Oosterbeek, which forms its western suburb. Here by Wednesday, September 20th, Major-General Urquhart had by strenuous effort at last established a perimeter of defence. The western half consisted of a detachment of glider pilots, the remnants of three companies of the Border Regiment, some Poles and a number of Royal Engineers. It was commanded by Brigadier Hicks.

The eastern half was made up of three glider pilot detachments, the Borderers, the Reconnaissance Squadron, the 21st Independent Parachute Company, elements of the Royal Army Service Corps who had abandoned the care of vehicles and stores and were fighting stoutly as infantry, all that remained of the 156th and 10th Parachute Battalions, and "Lonsdale Force," called after its Commander, Major R. T. H. Lonsdale, D.S.O., M.C., and made up of elements of the 1st, 3rd and 11th Parachute Battalions and the 2nd South Staffords. This eastern half was put under Brigadier Hackett, soon to be badly wounded. His place was taken by Lieutenant-Colonel I. Murray, the Commander of No. I Wing of the Glider Pilot Regiment. Such artillery as remained was concentrated north and south of Oosterbeek Church.

In this shrinking perimeter, of which the centre was roughly at Hartestein, where Headquarters were situated, the Division held out until the order to withdraw was received on Monday,

September 25th, and obeyed that night.

Within it all ranks fought with a gallant tenacity, equalled perhaps, but never surpassed by any soldiers of the British Army either now or at any other time in its long and honourable history. Here are a few of the many "moving accidents by Hood and field" and "hairbreadth escapes the imminent deadly breach" which occurred to every officer and man during those last grim days. There were the adventures of Lonsdale and his men near Oosterbeek Church. Lonsdale had been hit by a fragment of anti-aircraft shell just before jumping, but did not allow this handicap to interfere with his duties. Repeated enemy attacks on the church were beaten off, until his force was reduced to one Piat and one bomb. Then he withdrew to a nearby wood and there held out to the end. Among his men was the gallant Sergeant Walker of the South Staffords, who knocked out two tanks and was then wounded but, disregarding this mishap, seized a Bren gun and with it halted dead a German counter-attack, only to fall a victim shortly afterwards to the fire of a German tank.

North of the church Major R. Cain of the South Staffords and his company were fighting an equally stout battle. Soon after their arrival, and before occupying their new positions, they found a laundry where the men "had a wash and put on clean shirts which they found lying about."

Thus refreshed they took their stand on the high ground to the left of the church, a severe edifice with "a funeral inscription on the wall with some cherubs blowing trumpets round it." There they were soon repeatedly attacked by tanks and self-propelled guns, of which they knocked out some three or four.

A self-propelled gun which came into action every morning and afternoon was particularly troublesome. Cain determined to destroy it and fired some fifty bombs at it, his fire being directed by Captain Ian Meikle, who continued to do so till he was killed. Cain eventually entered a little shed with a Piat and two bombs, put his head round a corner of the door and seeing the gun, "fired at the thing and the bomb went off underneath it." The last shot of the gun blew the shed to pieces just after Cain had left it. Hardly had he disposed of the self-propelled gun when a tank came up the road. He crept towards it, waited till it was less than a hundred yards away, and then fired the Piat. The tank fired back immediately, and "this raised a huge cloud of dust and smoke. As soon as I could see the outline of the tank I let it have another. This also raised a lot of dust again, and through it I saw the crew of the tank baling out." They were dealt with by a Bren gun.

Cain fired a last shot to make sure, but the bomb burst prematurely in the muzzle of the Piat, wounding him in the face, perforating an eardrum and giving him two black eyes.

"I' THE IMMINENT, DEADLY BREACH"

Major F. A. S. Murray. of the Glider Pilot Regiment carried on the fight until wounded in the throat. Undaunted he led a successful counter-attack, and only then went to hospital, where he soon found himself in enemy hands. This did not suit him : after having his wound dressed, he walked out, "quite unarmed and in broad daylight," and made his way back to the Division. Major Bush of the 3rd Parachute Battalion behaved in similar fashion, breaking out of captivity to rejoin and then command a section of the perimeter. This, though again wounded, he held till the order to withdraw came.

It cannot too often be pointed out that the enemy mortar fire was of the most deadly kind. Our own, though not so heavy for lack of ammunition, also did great execution. The mortars maintained in action by Lieutenant H. R. Holman of the Border Regiment were especially well fought until all were destroyed together with most of their crews. When the last round had been tired and last mortar silenced, Holman collected all who were still on their feet and they fought on as infantry.

Captain R. R. Temple, G.S.O. III to the 4th Parachute

Brigade, fought for most of the time one-handed, his right arm having been smashed on the morning of the 20th. His shooting with a revolver held in his left hand was "most accurate." Captain J. W. Walker, a gunner, ended as adjutant to Payton-Reid, taking over his new duties on return from a two-day visit to hospital, whither he had been sent by a bullet which had perforated his steel helmet and the top of his head. Sergeant J. N. Smith kept his Bren gun in action after an enemy shell had knocked down the house on top of him.

Signalman R. M. Duguid had two jeeps shot under him, the second of which he repaired, under heavy fire. Private J. Steele of the Border Regiment became a purveyor of gammon bombs, retrieving these dangerous and useful weapons from a container which had been seen to fall in a sniper-haunted wood, just before an enemy tank attack developed.

The non-combatants vied with the fighting men in gallantry and devotion to duty. Private J. C. Proudfoot, a stretcher-bearer, "repeatedly we out into the open in full view to dress the casualties and drag them safety" : Captain R. T. Watkins, Chaplain to the 1st Parachute Battalion, was always "where the need was most great" and saved the lives of large numbers of the wounded. These deeds, chosen at random from files bright with similar reports on the actions of men equally brave, embroider a deathless tale and explain how it was that Oosterbeek continued to be defended long after it had by all the canons of war become untenable. The account them must end with the most remarkable of all, the exploits of Lance-Sergeant J. D. Baskeyfield of the South Staffordshire Regiment.

On September 20th, not long after the perimeter was formed, a fierce attack on Oosterbeek was launched by the enemy. Sergeant Baskeyfield was in command of a section manning a six-pounder anti-tank gun. Fighting it with the utmost "coolness and daring" they destroyed two Tiger tanks and a self propelled gun, holding their fire to make sure of success until the enemy were less than a hundred yards off. The sergeant and his crew did not escape unscathed. All were killed or wounded, Baskeyfield being badly hit in the leg. Refusing to be carried to the Regimental Aid Post, he remained alone with the gun and soon afterwards repelled a second and even fiercer armoured attack. "By this time" reports his Commanding Officer "his activity was the main factor in keeping the enemy tanks at bay. Of this the enemy themselves soon became aware for their fire destroyed his gun ; but the sergeant crawled- he could not walk-under intense fire to another close at hand, of which all the crew were dead, and brought single handed into action. He fired but two rounds and caused a self propelled gun to come to an abrupt halt. But the tank behind it fired and Sergeant Baskeyfield fell dead beside his second six pounder. For these deeds he was awarded a posthumous Victoria Cross, and his best epitaph is to be found in the words with which the citation ends. "During the remaining days at Arnhem stories of his valour were a constant inspiration to all ranks."

THE TENACITY OF THE GUNNERS

In all this heavy fighting the guns under the Commander of the Roy Artillery, Lieutenant-Colonel R. G. Loder-Symonds D.S.O., M.C., played a conspicuous part. Fifteen out of sixteen of the seventy-five mm. guns arrived safely with the first lift, and their numbers grew to twenty-one out a possible twenty four after the second lift had come in. They were put to the most strenuous use, on the first day firing forty rounds a gun, on the second fifty ; but shortage of ammunition made it impossible to maintain this rate in the later stages. Most of the guns were served in the firing line itself, and sometimes in advance of it. Their fire was directed by a number of forward observation officers posted in various points of vantage. Here Lieutenant J W Widdicombe held on for twenty-four hours directing a battery which broke up a heavy attack of the enemy, though the building on which he stood was shot to pieces all round him and he was compelled to continue his task perched on its wreckage.

"C " troop of the 2nd Battery was attacked on September 24th by a Tiger tank and a self-propelled gun at a range of 150 yards. The crews were prevented from firing their guns by heavy machine-gun fire, but Lieutenant A. Donaldson, with Lance-Bombardier Dickson, ran across a hundred yards of open ground and manned a six-pounder anti-tank gun, of which the crew had been killed. This the two men brought into action, but after firing eight or nine rounds the gun received a direct hit from the tank, which stunned Donaldson. On coming to, he and his bombardier made their way back to one of the guns of "C" troop and maintained it in action until all the ammunition was expended. Dickson then sought and found a Piat and with this weapon went on with the battle.

That same day Sergeant Daly of "B" troop temporarily dazed a Tiger tank with two shots tired at a range of a hundred yards. A second Tiger, attempting to pass the first, jolted it, whereupon it started into life again and opened heavy machine-gun fire against the sergeant and his anti-tank gun.

Everyone dived for cover, but Sergeant Daly crawled back to the gun, laid it, and sent the tank up in flame with his first round. Such deeds as these show the tenacity with which the guns were fought and the determination and skill with which the traditions of the Royal Regiment of Artillery were maintained by men taking their pieces into action by means and in circumstances very novel to war.

So the fight or rather the siege went on. There was no thought of giving up, even though the chances of relief dwindled with every day that passed.

As late as September 24th, Browning in Nijmegen received a message from Urquhart containing the stout-hearted words "resistance will be continued and we will do our best."

WHY RELIEF NEVER CAME

Why was the Division not relieved ? Why had no unit of the 2nd Army reached the bridge within the planned period of forty-eight hours ? Why, as day after day passed by, did they still linger ? The answer is simple. To reach Arnhem the 2nd Army had to thrust out a long, narrow armoured spearhead, and the units composing it, headed by the Guards Armoured Division, could use but one road, which splits into two soon after leaving the Nijmegen Bridge and joins together again near that of Arnhem. It is a road to advance along which is almost impossible if an enemy wishes to intervene ; for it runs first through orchards of plum and apple with distant poplars decorating the skyline, and then through flat, marshy fields extending to the banks of the Lower Rhine, and it is raised on a causeway some three or four feet above the surrounding country. No tank or armoured vehicle can leave it and not become bogged and, since large stretches are under observation from higher ground, it can be shelled at will as long as that ground remains uncaptured. It was never continuously under Allied control nor free from the enemy's fire. Sometimes it was cut for hours on end ; sometimes the point of the spearhead was blunted by frontal counter attacks. That in a word was why the 1st Airborne Division was not relieved.

Conditions along the road leading through Grave and Nijmegen to the outskirts of Arnhem can be gauged by what happened to Flight Lieutenant Turner, D.F.C., the pilot of a Stirling employed in dropping supplies to the airborne troops. On September 21st he was shot down near Nijmegen and presently arrived there on foot with his crew. Here they were given food, a three-ton lorry, and an order to make for Eindhoven. Five miles from that town they were told that two German tanks - Panthers, it was thought-and a body of S.S. troops were moving against the road from the north-east and would arrive at any moment. "We had two revolvers and a Sten gun between the nine of us," said Turner. Judging this armament insufficient with which to attack tanks, the party drove to Veghel, a small village close by, where they presently fell in with "an Army Lieutenant and three Bofors guns." All at once returned to the main road, determined to fight their way through.

The opportunity to do so soon arrived, for the German tanks made straight for them. The first was knocked out by the Bofors firing at a range of 400 yards, but in the ensuing battle with the second and the S.S. infantry accompanying it, the Army Lieutenant became a casualty, two of the three Bofors were destroyed, and the available ammunition for the third fell to fourteen rounds. So the crew of the Stirling moved off the road once more and joined some thirty British infantry who were without officers but had machine-guns. Though lacking all experience in ground warfare, Turner at once took command. Tiger tanks, suddenly appearing, drove the party back to Veghel, where the lorry, into which they had all clambered, was ambushed and destroyed. Undismayed, the survivors lined a ditch by the roadside, held off the enemy for ten hours with small-arms tire till darkness fell, and then retired with their wounded to a neighbouring house, whose owner gave them all the food he had-one slice of bread and butter and one apple to each man. By then there was almost no ammunition left, and they therefore lay quiet listening to the Germans fifty yards away, who, badly mauled, made no further attack. Late in the next afternoon the advanced guards of the leading British armoured division arrived, and Flight Lieutenant Turner was able to hand over his command, abandon fighting on land, and return eventually to the air, a more familiar element.

CAPTURE OF THE GREAT BRIDGE AT NIJMEGEN

Such an incident as this shows how fluid and uncertain was the battle raging in the stretch of country separating the British 1st Airborne Division in Arnhem from their American allies and comrades farther south, who were eventually able to make and retain contact with the main body of the 2nd Army. For the Americans had succeeded in all their allotted tasks. By September 19th the 101st Division had seized and was securely holding the bridge at Grave over the Maas, while the 82nd was fighting with magnificent gallantry to capture and hold the great bridge at Nijmegen over the Waal.

On that day, supported by the Guards Armoured Division, it fought one of the fiercest actions of the whole war, having by then been reinforced by the second lift carried in some 400 gliders, which landed within a few hundred yards of the front line.

For twenty-four hours the battle raged with great fury, but the Americans accomplished the seemingly impossible by crossing the Waal in assault boats under withering fire, and eventually seized the northern end of the bridge.

At the same time the Guards attacked the southern end, and soon success crowned the Allied arms. The great tanks roared across the bridge and their crews joined hands with the gallant American parachutists who had judged no price too high for victory. But that was the limit of accomplishment.

Farther north the 2nd Army could not push. Throughout, Lieutenant-General Browning had been in charge of the battle, directing it, first from woods and copses and then from a white house on the outskirts of Nijmegen, where he had arrived with his staff by glider on D day.

It will be remembered that the intention had been to drop most of the Polish Parachute Brigade on a zone immediately south of the bridge at Arnhem. As soon as it was realized that only its northern end was in our hands the zone was moved farther to the west and the Poles eventually landed on the 21st near Driel. Great efforts were then made to take them across the river to reinforce their hard-pressed British comrades. Lieutenant D. Storrs of the Royal Engineers, for example, with tired detachments taken out of the line from all Sapper units in turn, tried for four nights running to ferry them across. On the first night he was quite unable to do so and not a man landed on the other side. On the second night he brought over sixty Poles in rubber dinghies, crossing the river twenty-three times before dawn.

Altogether some 250 Poles passed the river and formed a valuable re-inforcement to the north-eastern corner of the defence. Here they fought with their proverbial gallantry.

Two hundred and fifty men of the Dorsetshire Regiment, part of the 43rd (Wessex) Division, also made most determined efforts to reach Urquhart's men. On the evening of September 22nd, after fighting most of the day, they reached the bank of the river, covering the last ten perilous miles at high speed in lorries, for they knew that behind them the Tiger tanks of the enemy, who had once more broken through, were in cumbersome but determined pursuit. Major H. Parker set booby traps for the Tigers and covered the approaches to the banks with Piats, while the rest of the Dorsets strove to cross the river in "Ducks " (amphibious vehicles) laden with stores and ammunition.

The ground at this point, however, was most unsuitable. The Ducks slithered off the road into the dyke and not one was successfully launched.

On the next day assault boats were used, the battalion carrying them 600 yards through an orchard under heavy mortar and machine-gun fire. Many were hit before they were launched, but a number took the water and into them climbed the men of Dorset. Some, caught in a swift current in midstream, were swept downwards towards the sea ; others were hit and sunk, but by daylight the elements of four companies were on the other side. There, however, they could do little, for they were at once pinned down by heavy tire. They sought to move to higher ground immediately above the river bank and not far from Oosterbeek, but to reach it they had to climb a slope of sixty degrees. The platoon in the van was led by the commanding officer of the battalion, Lieutenant-Colonel G. Tilly. He was last heard shouting " There they are ! Get at them with the bayonet ! " Then he disappeared, and no trace has been found of him.

All that day the Dorsets fought on in scattered groups, and at one time Major J. D. Grafton called on the guns of the 2nd Army to put down a concentration on his own position which was then filled with the enemy. The shooting was very effective, but neither the Poles nor the Dorsets were able to reach the Airborne Division in numbers large enough to alter the course of the battle. It continued to hold out in its perimeter in conditions which daily, hourly, grew worse.

FIFTEEN MORTAR BOMBS A MINUTE

They were, in fact, almost intolerable to all but troops determined to hold out to the last. Enemy fire varied in intensity, but never by day or night did it cease, though there was apt to be a lull at Sundown. "The Germans always drew stumps at seven o'clock," says Major Wilson. But he adds, "They mortared us continuously at all other times." It was this mortar fire which was especially galling and which accounted for a high proportion of the casualties suffered. Never could anyone feel reasonably safe even in a well-dug and well-sited slit trench. More than one "looked very like a grave," and more than one became a grave. On one small sector alone five mortar bombs fell every twenty seconds, and this rate of fire was often kept up by the enemy for hours at a time.

It would be wrong to maintain that this bombardment had no effect on the spirits of Urquhart's men. It had. As day succeeded day and no relief appeared, and ammunition ran lower and lower till there was almost none at all, to remain cheerful needed a constant effort of the will. The remedy- one which never failed- was to take some action against the enemy.

Sniping became a favourite pastime; and since the standard

of marksmanship was high, very few bullets were wasted. "We built a figure out of a pillow with a helmet stuck on one end of it," says Sergeant Quinn of the Reconnaissance Squadron, "and put it on the top of a broom handle. We popped this out now and again, always from a different window, so as to attract German snipers. One of us was watching them from a nearby house -not the house where we were using the dummy. Whenever a sniper showed up, he fired and got him. One of our chaps got fifteen like this, and I got two or three. We were using Stens and Brens. For this work it is best to fire single shots."

Wilson's Independent Parachute Company cut notches on the butts of their rifles for every German killed. One of them returned to England with eighteen. Others stalked tanks and self-propelled guns with Piats. Others, again, who had orders to issue and plans to make, stuck to their task, not allowing the heavy fire to interfere with its fulfilment, and even finding time to note the symptoms which that fire produced. "I found that under such long periods of mortar fire," says Lieutenant-Colonel Mackenzie, G.S.O.1 to the Division, who was to win a D.S.O., "my mind showed a tendency towards lethargy. It was hard to concentrate, and to write anything took a long time." On occasion there would be a lull and the tired men were able to relax for a few precious moments. "In the evening I would go to my trench," said one of them, and smoke a pipe. I used to look at an apple tree which grew nearby and had red apples on it and then I watched the stars come up." Near that spot some 350 years before, another poet, the gentle Philip Sidney, had watched those same stars as he lay dying of a mortal wound.

THE R.A.M.C. STAYS AT ITS POST

The wounded were looked after with great devotion by surgeons who remained at their posts to the last and entered captivity or death with them.

The 16th Parachute Field Ambulance, under Lieutenant-

Colonel E. Townsend, M.C., was established in the St. Elizabeth Hospital on the evening of the first day, but the Germans reoccupied the buildings a few hours later and took prisoner all the unit save two surgeons, Major Longland and Captain Lipmann-Kessell, who used the greatest ingenuity in preventing their enforced departure. On several occasions when German soldiers arrived with orders to move them, they at once began fresh surgical operations which even the S.S. men were loath to disturb. The two officers remained in the hospital for some weeks until all the wounded there were fit to be taken with them into captivity. The chief medical dressing station was a house not within the perimeter at all but just outside it. Here many of those wounded in the early days of the action were tended. Fighting went on all round this hospital and more than once threatened to invade it. At one p.m. on September 23rd, for example, a German officer under a large Red Cross flag, approached Brigadier Hackett and "threatened that unless our troops withdrew from the house, he would be forced to blow the M.D.S. to pieces. Half an hour later, however, he agreed not to do so provided we did not fire from the immediate vicinity of the hospital." On the next day these threats were renewed, although the Germans were well aware that their own wounded to the number of 150 or more were being cared for by the same doctors.

Eventually many of the wounded, both German and English, were taken by the enemy back into Arnhem. A Regimental Aid Post was established by Captain Martin in Oosterbeek. Conditions in it were very bad, for it was soon housing upwards of 200 wounded, and little beyond first aid could be given to them. The owner of the house, a Dutch lady, worked without rest or food, helped by a boy of seventeen who did likewise. What water there was had to be brought from a pump close by, till it ran "red with blood."

Every evening the lady moved from room to room, her bible in her hand, and in the light of a torch read aloud the 91st Psalm, "for," said she, "it has comforted my children and may comfort you." Lying on mattresses or straw amid the stench of wounds and death, the men heard "her soft voice speaking most carefully the words of King David, 'Thou shalt not be afraid for the terror by night, nor for the arrow that flieth by day, nor for the pestilence that walketh in darkness, nor for the destruction that wasteth at noonday '."

Fire, thirst and hunger were among the tribulations grimly endured. As time wore on, more and more of the houses, so stoutly defended, were set ablaze and became untenable. Hit by a phosphorus bomb, a house usually began to burn in earnest some five minutes later, and this short interval gave to those holding it just time to move to another. After the first forty-eight hours, food became very short, and towards the end was entirely lacking. The Germans cut off the town water supply, and to the pangs of hunger those of thirst were added. "We went four days without food," says Sergeant Quinn, "but we could still get water from a well." In this he and those with him were luckier than most. There were vegetables in the gardens- potatoes, cabbages and some tomatoes -but without water it was difficult to cook them. There were apples to be had from the trees, and some men of the 156th Parachute Battalion "found a bakery and had bread and bottled cherries." The 21st Independent Parachute Company were more fortunate than many of their fellows. "We lived," its commander reports, "on two meals a day, mostly of tinned vegetables. Once a kid ran across the lawn of my headquarters and we killed and ate it."

The cellars of certain houses were found to contain small stocks of food and occasionally of wine, "Champagne, Graves, a light claret and Bols gin." One company filled a bath half full of water before the tap failed and used this for cooking, even after a piece of the ceiling had fallen into it and made it look like "thin; unpleasant porridge." "There just weren't any army rations after the first day," reports an officer, "but there were some tame rabbits, one of which I fed. He used to scratch at the wire of his hutch as I went by, and I'd give him a leaf of lettuce or cabbage. One day a parachutist on the scrounge walked off with my rabbit, dead .... I made him hand it over and left it between my batman's trench and mine, where it got blown to pieces by a shell. Chickens didn't seem to mind the mortaring at all. They lost a few feathers but went on pecking and scratching about quite calmly." Such food as fell from the air went to the Regimental Aid Posts.

"THEY FLEW STRAIGHT INTO A FLAMING HELL"

Why food and ammunition were not dropped in quantities large enough to keep so comparatively small a body of men supplied is a question which may pertinently be asked. The answer forms a short, tragic, glorious chapter in the history of the Royal Air Force. A zone north west of Arnhem, in the area of Warnsborn, had been chosen as the place on which supplies were to be dropped. Had it been possible to form the perimeter outside the town in accordance with the original plan, this zone would have been well within the lines of the defence. But it was not. As has already been explained the high ground near the zone was never captured, and both remained in the hands of the enemy. A message explaining this was sent by wireless, and a new zone nearer to Oosterbeek indicated. The message with this vital alteration was not received in time. Indeed the great lack of communication between the 1st Airborne Division and Lieutenant General Browning, fighting a hard and successful battle to the south on the Maas and Waal, was more than an inconvenience and sometimes as much as a disaster. This was especially so where the Royal Air Force was concerned. The fact that this extremely important message did not get through, though it was several times repeated, meant that the supply aircraft, Stirlings for the most part together with unarmoured Dakotas, dropped their precious burdens, not upon the airborne troops, but upon their enemies. More than that, to do so they had to encounter very heavy anti-aircraft fire of which the accuracy, since they had to fly low, was high. Unfalteringly they met it.

"Arnhem, 19th September, 1630 hours, " runs the war diary of the Division. "Re-supply dropped on pre-arranged S.D.P. ' V. ' (Supply Dropping Point) which was in enemy's hands. Yellow smoke, yellow triangles and every conceivable means were used to attract attention of pilots and get them to drop supplies within our lines ; this had very limited success." It had indeed. The weather was misty, but the arranged dropping point could be seen and the pilots had eyes for nothing else. "My most poignant memory, " writes Lieutenant-Colonel M. St. J. Packe, in charge of the Royal Army Service Corps elements in Oosterbeek, "will always be the time I spent watching the supply aircraft coming over and dropping their containers on an area not under our control .... They were met by a screen of flak, and it was awe-inspiring to see them fly straight into it, straight into a flaming hell. We thought that some would not face it and would jettison their cargoes, in which case we should get them, for they would fall short and therefore in our lines ; but they all stuck to their course and went on, nor did they hesitate. " A Stirling and a Dakota were seen that day, both on fire, circling round the zone. They were doomed and their pilots knew it, but they might still drop their supplies on the right spot. To do so immediately, however, might interfere with those more fortunate than themselves who were timed to arrive a moment or two before them. So they held off, awaiting their turn. It came, and they went in, blazing, to release the containers ; before they fell "like two torches from the sky," they had done all in their power to ensure success. Such cold-blooded courage is the extreme of heroism. It was prompted, not merely by a strong sense of duty, but also by a feeling of comradeship with those fighting a doughty and perilous battle in the Woods beneath which "looked so quiet and clean," but were full of strife and carnage.

THE LAST HOURS OF RESISTANCE

One of the crew of a Stirling, badly hit but still able to fly, looked back at the dropping zone he had just left. "I could see black puffs round the aircraft behind us," he notes in his diary. "It must have been a terrible spot to be in, and we were glad to get out of it. I wondered what sort of battle the airborne men were having and knew it must be tough ; but they had guts and plenty of them. We all wanted to do everything we could to help them." This indeed the Royal Air Force did, as the losses in aircraft testify. On September 18th, the first day on which supplies were dropped, they were six per cent., on the 19th eight per cent., and on the 21st twenty per cent. The average loss during the six days on which flying was possible- on two it was not- was somewhat more than seven per cent. This, though not crippling, was severe. Among the casualties was the leader of the supply aircraft, Wing Commander Davis, D.S.O., who had inspired his crews with a spirit of resolution equal to his own. It is grievous to record that only 7.4 per cent. of the total number of tons dropped was collected by the beleaguered division. For, after the evening of the fifth day, that was what the airborne troops were. "No knowledge of elements of Division in Arnhem for twenty-four hours. Balance of Division in very tight perimeter. Heavy mortaring and machine-gun fire .... Our casualties heavy. Rations stretched to utmost. Relief within twenty-four hours vital. " This is the entry made at 9.44 p.m. on Thursday, September 21st, in the Divisional diary. Yet they held on for another four days. As these went by, it became more and more difficult to move about inside the perimeter. Snipers were active, persistent and ubiquitous, and all the roads were blocked by trunks and branches of trees, bricks and masonry strewn over their surface.

At all times communication between Major-General Urquhart and his Chief, Lieutenant-General Browning, was difficult and often impossible. A large number of the wireless sets carried into action were damaged either on landing or subsequently by enemy action ; a large number were unserviceable almost from the beginning. Throughout the time he spent at the Headquarters of the 1st Parachute Brigade on the outskirts of Arnhem, Urquhart was out of touch for many hours with the 2nd Battalion at the bridge and his own headquarters at Hartestein, though the distance between was not large and was well within the range of the standard equipment carried.

By noon on September 22nd, Urquhart judged it indispensable to send two officers across the Lower Rhine to acquaint Browning with the situation. For this purpose he chose Lieutenant-Colonels C. B. Mackenzie, his G.S.O.1, and E. C. Myers, C.B.E., D.S.O., who was commanding the Royal Engineers. These officers made the crossing under enemy fire in a rubber boat, in company with two others. The boat was inflated in a building at Oosterbeek and dragged over the fields till the river was reached. "I rowed," says Colonel Mackenzie, "and Myers steered .... We parked the boat in a little bay and crawled away from the bank .... There was a battle going on and we couldn't make out which were Poles and which were Germans."

Having found Polish Headquarters, they made what arrangements they could for the Polish Parachute Brigade to be ferried over, but no one was very hopeful, for there was a great lack of boats or materials from which rafts could be built. That evening Mackenzie set off to find the G.O.C.

He went in a reconnaissance car and presently drew near to a windmill, round the corner of which poked "a dirty-looking green nose." It belonged to a Tiger tank, which went at once into action and at the end of the encounter Mackenzie found himself with the reconnaissance car upside down in a ditch.

He crawled away and after some time two Sherman tanks arrived and cleared a passage, so that he was able eventually to speak with General Browning between ten and eleven the next morning. The return journey was made without incident, and he reported to General Urquhart that night, having concerted plans for an evacuation now seen to be inevitable.

"These things befell at Arnhem"

It took place on the night of September 25th/26th, and began at ten p.m.

The wounded at Divisional Headquarters were left under the care of Lieutenant Randall, R.A.M.C. All doctors and chaplains still alive remained at the Dressing Stations and Regimental Aid Posts. The orders issued were to make as little noise as possible and to reach the river bank in the general area of Oosterbeek, where sappers with assault boats would ferry them across, a distance of between 100 and 150 yards. Many of the men bound pieces of cloth, obtained from houses or from their own uniforms, about their boots, and as soon as it was dark what remained of the Division moved off. The Germans were tired but suspicious. A heavy bombardment, carried out by the guns of the 2nd Army to cover the withdrawal, seems to have been regarded by them as designed to cover the passage of the river in strength by reinforcements. A number of German machine-guns in the woods or on the edge of the fields near Oosterbeek caused a certain amount of confusion. "We heard a German challenge," says one account, "and then a second or two later a blaze of light some fifty yards away, into which, after moving to a flank, we Hung hand grenades."

Soon a queue was forming on the river bank, waiting, in a night jet-black and streaming with rain, for the infantry assault boats, each of which could hold fourteen or fifteen men. A battery of A.A. guns sent red tracer shells across the river to mark the place at which the passage was to be made. They belonged to the Wessex Division and fired a round every minute, alternately in pairs, for seven hours. It was, of necessity, impossible to move them, and each tracer shell that stabbed the darkness betrayed their position. There were too many troops for the boats, some of which were very rickety. Moreover, though comparatively calm near both of its banks, the Lower Rhine was running strongly in the middle.

"We got into a boat," says Lieutenant-Colonel St. J. Packe, "pushed off, and soon reached that part of the river where the current was flowing strongly. I thought that, once in its grip, we would be swept along into what seemed to me to be a hellish battle in progress downstream. At that moment the outboard engine cut, so we seized our rifles and paddled with the butts. I beat time. Those without rifles encouraged those with them until they were persuaded to swop." Many, unable to find a place in the boats, or eager to yield it to a comrade in more evil case than their own, preferred to swim the river. Among them was Siely, the Regimental Sergeant-Major of the Light Regiment. He stayed behind to help late-comers, and it was broad daylight before he began the passage. "I stripped completely," he said, "because I had just seen three men drown, weighed down by their clothes." He got safely across and then made for an old house not far from the south bank, where he assisted his Commanding Officer, who was in the same condition as himself, to assume a lady's blouse. He himself chose "a lady's very nice dark cloth coat."

By noon on September 27th the long ordeal was over. The Division, which had started 10,095 strong, including the glider pilots, had by then lost 7,605 officers and men in killed, wounded and missing. Now at last it was at Nijmegen ; and there, in a large red-brick school in a quiet tree-bordered thoroughfare, an issue of tea, rum, food, and one blanket a man was made. Some who had arrived earlier in the day received a less formal welcome from the sea-borne elements of the Division, who were awaiting them, having advanced some 700 miles through France, Belgium and Holland. Captain Scott Malden, for example, one of the Divisional Intelligence officers, reached Headquarters clad in several yards of flannel secured by a belt. He was given a breakfast which consisted of half a tumbler of Cointreau, a large bowl of Irish stew, and then a small glass of the same liqueur. After this he slept without moving for twelve hours. Others were provided with the like good cheer, and soon that school at Nijmegen, set aside for their reception, was echoing with the voices of weary men who had passed through an ordeal few have been called upon to face in this war or in any other. They had suffered much, they were weary beyond measure, but they were sustained by that most potent aid to recovery, the knowledge that they had done all and more than their duty.

THEY WALKED BACK TO FREEDOM

Behind them, on the other side of the turbid stream, many of their comrades still remained. These belonged to those elements of the Division who had penetrated deeply into Arnhem in an effort to reinforce the 2nd Parachute Battalion at the head of the bridge. Many of them were lying wounded or dead in Arnhem and its outskirts ; many were prisoners, captured in the wrecks of burning houses, their ammunition spent ; but many were wandering among the woods or farms, or hiding in the back streets of the little town. They lived there for weeks, cared for by the Dutch, who to do so showed a spirit of cunning, fortitude and courage which may justly be called sublime.

A great number succeeded in making then way back days and weeks later to the British line. Among them was Brigadier Lathbury, the Commander of the 1st Parachute Brigade. He, it will be remembered, had on his own urgent representations been left wounded and half paralysed in a small house on the outskirts of Arnhem. Its inhabitants took him to the local hospital outside the defensive perimeter. There he was cared for by British surgeons and Dutch nurses, though the enemy was in control. In a day or two he had recovered sufficiently to be able to hobble, and as soon as he realized that the plan had failed and that the 2nd Army would not arrive to capture the town, he crept away at midnight into the woods, walking on a compass bearing in what he hoped was the direction of freedom.

Presently he fell in with a private soldier, and for the best part of a week they remained in the woods, sleeping in a shed and constantly on the move. Another week went by, and he was then put into contact with Mayor A D Tatham-Warter of the 2nd Parachute Battalion, who had been captured by the Germans, escaped from a dressing station, and deliberately returned in order to organise the escape of as many of the Division as could be found still at large. Tatham-Warter showed great aplomb, moving about the district quite freely and so bearing himself that it seemed that the Germans did not suspect him. Once he arrived at the door of a house at the same time as two German soldiers. He glanced sharply at them. They stood aside and allowed him to go in first.

Tatham-Warter and Lathbury fell in with Lieutenant-Colonel Dobie, commanding the 1st Parachute Battalion, and the three men made various plans. Because of the importance of the information he possessed, Dobie was sent ahead and eventually succeeded in making his way with the utmost difficulty to the 2nd Army and safety. The others waited several days and collected stragglers from all over the place. Matters were complicated by the fact that the Germans had decided to evacuate the entire civil population.

The day of the evacuation was that chosen by Lathbury and Tatham-Warter as that on which the parachutists should make their escape. "Our plan worked perfectly .... Eighty officers and men who had been hiding in the area were all assembled at the rendezvous .... To reach it, Tatham-Warter and I cycled along the road side by side, and every time we saw a German- and we passed at least 200, some in groups, some in platoons marching along- I expected to be challenged, but nothing untoward happened."

Forty more other ranks commanded by Major Hibbert, Brigade Major of the 1st Parachute Brigade, were too far away to reach the rendezvous in time, so they were taken there in two lorries. "During the journey they wore their uniforms, carried their weapons and lay flat on the floor of the lorries. They drove straight to the rendezvous, and as they de-bussed, German troops were walking past them on the road." Eventually the whole party reached the bank of the Lower Rhine, and after an anxious forty-five minutes, during which they had a brush with the Germans who evidently mistook them "for a strong patrol," got back across the river aided by the fire of tracer shells.

TWELVE DAYS IN A CUPBOARD

The adventures of Major A. G. Deane-Drummond, M.C., were even more remarkable. He belongs to the Royal Corps of Signals, and first saw active service as a parachutist in the attack on the aqueduct in Southern Italy in 1941. Taken prisoner then, he twice escaped and eventually came back to his old Division. When they flew to the capture of Arnhem he jumped with the 1st Parachute Battalion, and after a time was sent on to discover, if he could, what was wrong with the wireless sets, for no messages were being received by Divisional Headquarters. He succeeded in putting right those in use at Brigade, then joined a party of forty men in the attack, already described, on the Pavilion near the river.

Long and continuous fighting reduced the numbers of this small force trying to break through to the bridge, and Deane-Drummond eventually found himself alone with his batman in a deserted house. As they were exploring it, a large party of Germans arrived, most of them belonging to an S.S. unit. They put snipers in the upper rooms, and to make sure that they would not desert their posts, locked the doors. In the meanwhile Deane-Drummond and his batman had gone to ground in the water closet, where they spent the next forty-eight hours. Its door they fastened, and the handle was frequently tried from the outside. No attempt, however, was made to force a way in. Occasionally the Germans lapse into good manners.

When the fighting died away, the two parachute soldiers crept out of their hiding place, muffled their boots with their battle blouses, and crept down the stairs and out of the house, where they separated, intending to meet on the other side of the Lower Rhine. They never did so. Deane-Drummond stripped, tied his clothes in his waterproof jumping smock, and swam the river. After dressing, he began to make his way towards the railway bridge, through an orchard and across some fields. There were Germans all about him, for he could hear them coughing and talking. He went through several lines of slit trenches and had almost reached the railway embankment near the bridge when he fell headlong into a trench on to a German soldier.

Deane-Drummond blew the man's brains out, but "as I lay on top of him another German sprang on me. It seemed certain that I was to be shot, but I suppose the second man did not know his comrade was dead and did not fire for fear of hurting him. Instead of being killed I was made a prisoner."

He did not remain one for very long. Taken back to Arnhem, he watched his opportunity and made off while other parachutists were being rounded up. The refuge he chose was the nearest house, which proved to his misfortune to be some kind of German headquarters. He had just time to bolt into a large, strongly made Dutch cupboard before some S.S. officers entered the room and began to interrogate a number of prisoners. Deane-Drummond spent twelve days in that cupboard, with nothing to eat but a piece of bread and nothing to drink but the contents of his water bottle. At long last another chance came and he slipped away and hid in the garden, being by this time, as he reports, "not a little exhausted." He remained a further three weeks on the wrong side of the Lower Rhine until at last he, too, got safely away.

The men of the parachute and air landing brigades who fell into the enemy's hands were most of them wounded. They were removed to Apeldoorn, and after some days departed thence on foot, or in cattle trucks, to captivity in the interior of the Reich. The wounded received neither food nor medical attention after the first forty-eight hours, when the doctors and the Dutch nurses of Arnhem, who had attended them with unselfish devotion, were no longer allowed to continue their ministrations. Those who survived the journey were deemed fit to work and were accordingly put to labour under blows and unprintable insults in lead-mines. Here they languished until the swift advent of the victorious Allies announced an end to their sufferings. For a moment, however, these were increased, for the prisoners found themselves once again on the march, or jolting in lorries, towards any part of Germany not yet captured. For many that dreadful journey was their last. What the enemy had failed to achieve at Arnhem with Spandaus, self-propelled guns, mortars, tanks, and all the armoury of modern war, he partially succeeded in accomplishing with hunger, thirst and cudgels along the dusty or muddy roads of Germany. For periods as long as fifteen days the men were given but one issue of food, and that consisted of ersatz bread, and more than one batch of prisoners received not even this meagre ration, but were compelled to rely on the non-existent charity of the native inhabitants, Nevertheless, when deliverance came, the courage of the survivors was found to be unbroken. Regimental Sergeant-Major J. C. Lord received his rescuers in a neatly pressed uniform with button bright and shining. His demeanour typifies the spirit that prevailed among the men of Arnhem.

In the treatment of their prisoners the Germans maintained, and enhanced, that reputation for infamous cruelty which they have been at pains to acquire in so many wars through so many centuries.

THE STRATEGIC VALUE OF ARNHEM

With tales of heroism and suffering such as these the story of the 1st Airborne Division in Holland must end ; but the story shows also that as a corporate whole this Division triumphantly vindicated the soundness of their training and proved beyond doubt or dispute that an airborne army is not a luxury but a necessity. On this ground alone the expedition was more than justified; on every other it was abundantly so. For consider the general position of the British armies in the west before and after the battle. Up to September 17th the enemy thought to profit from the tenacious resistance offered by his garrisons in Dunkirk, Lorient, St. Nazaire, and other great French ports. It was denying to the Allies certain links in the chain of supply of vital importance if the pressure of their armies was to be maintained. It seemed to the German High Command that they would be able to use the time thus gained to establish upon the Maas, the Waal and the Lower Rhine, three successive lines on which to stand and fight. They were in the full throes of preparing to do so when out of the skies, which Goering had once boasted would ever belong to the Luftwaffe, a blow fell with devastating suddenness. In the space not of days but of hours this scheme of defence collapsed. At one bound the British 2nd Army leapt nearly sixty miles towards the German frontier and became deeply ensconced in what the enemy had fondly hoped would be his front throughout the winter.

Before a week had passed, the Allies had secured all the bridges over two of the three rivers and possessed that most valuable of all assets in war, a firm base for future operations.

The enemy's reaction to the airborne attack, though immediate and violent, achieved no more than a limited success. As has been told, he could claim the recapture of the most northerly of the bridges and the thrusting back of the 1st Airborne Division with heavy casualties over the Lower Rhine. This is a fact which must be neither minimized nor exaggerated.

The loss of many gallant and highly trained men in an operation of great daring and much hazard must be set against the gain to the general conduct of the campaign as a whole. That this gain was very considerable, no one, not even the enemy, who was constrained to praise the conduct of the Division, will deny.

The resolute seizure of the bridge at Arnhem, which was under British control for three days, combined with the maintenance of a defensive position north of the river for nine days, forced the enemy to devote large resources, among them the remains of two S.S. Panzer Divisions, to the task of ejecting the audacious Urquhart and his men. Had the Germans not been under this necessity, their counter-attacks farther south against the American 82nd and 101st Divisions could have been pressed with much greater vigour and might possibly have succeeded, at least for a time. That they failed must be written largely on the credit side of the ledger when calculating the profit and loss incurred by the operation ; or, to vary the metaphor, because a duellist pierces the chest but not the heart of his adversary, he has not failed in his attack, for he has, none the less, inflicted a grievous, perhaps a mortal wound. For the British 6th and the 17th American Airborne Divisions was reserved the honour of inflicting it on the Germans less than six months later, north of Wesel on the other side of the Rhine. Their swift and overwhelming success would scarcely have been possible if the battle of Arnhem had not been fought.

They fought on, they fought on ...

As for the officers and men of the 1st Airborne Division, what they think of that battle is plain. " Thank you for the party," wrote Brigadier Hackett to General Urquhart afterwards. "It didn't go quite as we hoped and got a bit rougher than we expected. But speaking for myself, I'd take it on again any time and so, I'm sure, would everybody else." That he is right in his surmise no one who reads the story of the 1st Airborne Division at Arnhem can have any doubt. In the tranquil sunshine of an autumn afternoon, its officers and men descended upon territory held in force by the enemy. Some were in action while still falling or gliding through the air, and all were heavily engaged within an hour of landing. From that moment onwards not a man save the dead or desperately wounded but was continuously fighting both by day and by night. They fought in thick woods tearing aside the undergrowth to come to grips with the enemy ; they fought in well ordered streets, in neat houses, in town halls, in taverns, in churches- anywhere where a German was to be found.

With no weapon larger than a seventy five mm gun and for the most part only with Brens, gammon bombs and Piats, which can be carried and handled by one man unaided, they attacked Tiger tanks weighing fifty six tons and self propelled guns with a range of seven miles. Of these they destroyed or put out of action some sixty. The number of the enemy they killed or wounded is not exactly known, but it is not less than 7,000. With no reinforcements save the wounded, who, if their legs would still bear them, staggered back to the firing line, they fought on. With an enemy growing ever stronger, pressing against them on all sides but one- and that a wide, swiftly flowing river they fought on. Without sleep, presently without food or water, at the end almost without ammunition, they fought on. When no hope of victory remained, when all prospect of survival had vanished, when death alone could give them ease, they fought on. In attack most daring, in defence most cunning, in endurance most steadfast, they performed a feat of arms which will be remembered and recounted as long as the virtues of courage and resolution have power to move the hearts of men.

Now these things befell at Arnhem.

The British 1st Airborne paid a very heavy price for their courage in adversity. This iconic image encapsulates the British experience of the battle for Arnhem.